HENRY HOBSON RICHARDSON
AND HIS WORKS

Mariana Griswold Van Rensselaer

(MRS. SCHUYLER VAN RENSSELAER)

with a new introduction by
WILLIAM MORGAN

DOVER PUBLICATIONS, INC.

NEW YORK

This Dover edition, first published in 1969, is an unabridged republication of the work originally published in a limited edition of five hundred copies by Houghton, Mifflin and Company in 1888, to which has been added a new Introduction prepared especially for this reprint edition by William Morgan.

Standard Book Number: 486-22320-5
Library of Congress Catalog Card Number: 68-12915
Manufactured in the United States of America

Dover Publications, Inc.
180 Varick Street
New York, N.Y. 10014

INTRODUCTION TO THE DOVER EDITION

Henry Hobson Richardson is widely regarded as one of the giants of American architecture. Both a prophet of the future and a remnant of the past, he became the leader of the revival of Romanesque forms that bears his name, while at the same time his powerful buildings and imaginative use of materials influenced the generation of modern architects that succeeded him. Nonetheless, as the late Carroll Meeks demonstrated, Richardson was not the first to use Romanesque forms in this country, and although he is often included (with such men as Louis Sullivan and Frank Lloyd Wright) in lists of important early modern architects, Richardson was not a "modern" architect in the usual meaning of that term.

But if historians do not always agree on Richardson's place in American architecture, few would dispute the fact that Mariana Griswold Van Rensselaer's *Henry Hobson Richardson and His Works* is the foundation of all scholarship on the subject. First issued in an edition of five hundred copies by Houghton and Mifflin in 1888, two years after the architect's death, the factual treatment of Richardson's life and the illustrations of his work made her monograph the only comprehensive study of the architect until Henry Russell Hitchcock's *The Architecture of H. H. Richardson and His Times* appeared in 1936. In his book, Hitchcock acknowledges his own and future historians' debt to Mrs. Van Rensselaer's study, which remains unchallenged as the authoritative biography of the architect. Because the work has formerly been available only in the early limited edition, this reprint, which contains all the superb drawings and photographs, will be of unquestioned service to the student of American architecture.

If Richardson stands out as a giant figure in an age dominated by the masculine ethos, Mrs. Van Rensselaer deserves recognition as an all but unique personage of the Victorian era—a distinguished woman architectural critic. Born in 1851 and educated by private tutors and European travel, she turned to art and architectural criticism after her husband's death in 1884. An intelligent and well-read woman, she produced several books and articles on a wide range of subjects encompassing painting, gardening, poetry, and history, as well as architecture. Her books on art and architecture include such varied titles as *Book of American Figure Painters* and *American Etchers* (1886), *Six Portraits* (1889), and *English Cathedrals* (1887), which was instrumental in renewing American interest in English Gothic architecture, but probably her best-known work is the two-volume *History of the City of New York in the Seventeenth Century* (1909). Mrs. Van Rensselaer's uncommon breadth of interest is reflected in a life of public service as well as in her writings; she served as an inspector of New York City schools and was president of the Public Education Association of New York for seven years. Despite her active role in public affairs, she remained a gentlewoman, as is evidenced by her 1894 pamphlet *Should We Ask for the Suffrage?*, in which she strongly opposed giving women the vote. Although recognized in her lifetime by an honorary doctorate from Columbia University and honorary memberships in the American Institute of Architects and the American Society of Landscape Architects, Mrs. Van Rensselaer was neither an outstanding scholar nor a brilliant researcher. It can be said, however, that her books are, on the whole, well written, thorough, and accurate.

Not a few of the now familiar details of Richardson's life have come to us through *Henry Hobson Richardson and His Works*. The first seven chapters are straightforward biography and deal with Richardson's birth and background, his years of struggle in Paris, the important tour made with Phillips Brooks, his personal traits, and an interesting chapter on his hereditary influences, especially the intellectual heritage of his famous ancestor Dr. Joseph Priestley. The remainder of the book contains descriptions and discussions of Richardson's architectural works presented chronologically and grouped by major forms of buildings, executed or projected—a listing that remains, for the most part, accurate. Moreover, her personal appraisal of these works adds appreciably to the contribution made by the listing; here Mrs. Van Rensselaer offers the earliest assessment of Richardson's complete work, and many of this amateur architectural historian's points are still valid.

In judging Mrs. Van Rensselaer's comments, it should be remembered that the author was a personal friend of Richardson's and that such frequently quoted remarks as "The things I want most to design are a grain-elevator and the interior of a great river-steam-boat" (p. 22), were spoken to her. Despite her personal association with the architect, Mrs. Van Rensselaer exhibits no little objectivity. This lends credence to her critical comments, for on occasion she does not hesitate to criticize Richardson's less successful works. Of Brattle Square Church, she says: "the church is not, as a whole, a successful piece of work. No part of it is very interesting except the tower . . ." (p. 52). Of his early houses, the only one that she calls "successful as a whole" is the Watts Sherman house in Newport. Contemporary historians would probably concur with her opinion that Richardson's "early buildings, taken as a whole, do not foreshadow those whose list begins with Trinity Church" (p. 56), for this was the period when "Richardson was simply feeling his way."

One value of the proximity of the author to her subject is that in chronicling almost all of Richardson's work she includes drawings and descriptions of buildings and projects that were never executed, have since been destroyed, or are not remembered as important or admired examples of his work. The obviously important buildings are given more space (although one curious omission is the Stoughton house in Cambridge) and, fittingly, there is an entire chapter devoted to Trinity Church. The importance of Trinity Church as a pivotal work in Richardson's career, both stylistically and professionally, is well known, and Mrs. Van Rensselaer covers fully the dramatic changes in the design, which she considers emblematic of his constant self-criticism. In this connection the author is at pains to point out why, in her view, the tower of Trinity Church is not in fact copied from the photograph of that of the old cathedral at Salamanca, sent to Richardson by John La Farge, as is commonly supposed. In her defense of Richardson, Mrs. Van Rensselaer steals the wind from the sails of those who would dismiss most of Richardson's architecture, and Trinity Church is particular, as merely "eclectic" by simply stating: "I think it is hardly necessary to explain that it has never been part of an architect's duty to try to be original in the absolute meaning of the term, or that in these late days of art he could not be so even if he tried his best" (p. 64).

Using the same format, Mrs. Van Rensselaer runs through Richardson's other works: the small town libraries, the partially completed New York State Capitol at Albany, the City Hall in that same city, Sever and Austin Halls at Harvard, the Albany Cathedral competition and its disappointing result, the superb railroad stations (the importance of which she fully understands), the stone and shingle houses, and finally the great commercial and civic structures of Pittsburgh and Chicago. Only rarely does she depart from her objective tone to bestow accolades such as that accorded the Allegheny County Court House in Pittsburgh: "There is no other municipal building like Richardson's Court-house. It is as new as the needs it meets, as American as the community for which it was built. Yet it might stand without loss of prestige in any city in the world" (p. 93). Surely such praise was motivated by her knowledge of Richardson's feelings for the Pittsburgh work, but this is in contrast to a more typical and somewhat low-keyed description of another of Richardson's works, the Stone Bridge in Boston's Fenway. Although one of the architect's most delightful and thoroughly satisfying works, this is written of as "simply utilitarian in character" and "a thing of beauty as well as of very evident strength and serviceableness" (p. 72). Aside from occasional critical comments, Mrs. Van Rensselaer wisely avoids declarative value judgments of what to her were new buildings. This restraint is in considerable measure responsible for her book's continued relevance.

Mrs. Van Rensselaer's work is not without its faults, and, armed with hindsight, there are points with which one could easily take issue. But the author was a biographer, not a soothsayer. Her early efforts bequeathed to posterity a basic biography and a contemporary record of the works of an architect who left no writings of his own, and in this first major life of Richardson, Mrs. Van Rensselaer gave expression to the qualities of his art in a way that could hardly be improved upon (p. 112):

> Strength in conception; clearness in expression; breadth in treatment; imagination; and a love for repose and massive dignity of aspect, and often for an effect which in the widest meaning of the word we may call "romantic." The first is the most fundamental and important quality, and upon it depends to a very large degree the presence of the others.

The task of assessing Richardson's position in American architecture belonged not so much to Mrs. Van Rensselaer's generation as to ours, and any evaluation we might make most certainly will be re-evaluated and quite possibly modified by future generations. We can grant him his rightful place as the foremost exponent (but not the founder) of the Romanesque Revival—the so-called Richardson Romanesque. The point of Richardson's architecture is misunderstood by those who seek historical antecedents as the key to his works—it matters little that the spiky acanthus decorations on Austin Hall are reminiscent of those on San Vitale in Ravenna, nor is the wide nave of Trinity Church any more or any less successful if it is seen as a descendent of Vignola's Church of the Gesù. With a growing appreciation of Richardson's work there will doubtless come an understanding of the until recently much-maligned work of men who followed and imitated him, especially Bruce Price, William A. Potter, Halsey Wood, and Leroy Buffington. Their work, however "unmodern," should be judged, as Richardson's, on the basis of architectural quality and in the context of their time.

The other fashionable opinion of Richardson's importance, that of a pioneer of modern architecture, must also come before review. There can be no doubt that as a boldly utilitarian building stripped of all ornamentation and many historical preconceptions, Richardson's Marshall Field Warehouse strongly influenced modern commercial architecture and helped to prepare the way for the modern tall building. Nevertheless, the Marshall Field Warehouse still employed traditional methods of masonry construction, and much earlier other architects had used traditional elements to achieve a functional building of considerable distinction, as when during the period of the Greek Revival Alexander Parris had designed the Quincy Market in Boston.

Although Richardson himself never built skyscrapers or railroad bridges, his work exerted an influence beyond his immediate followers to the architects of such structures, who were particularly taken with his expressive use of materials—the essential qualities of stone and the picturesque effects achieved through the use of wood shingle. Unlike so many of his contemporaries, Richardson was able to conceive of a building as a whole and to maintain its integrity throughout, regardless of decorative features. This "organic" approach was one of his principal legacies to Sullivan and Wright. Richardson's powerful, individual style came at a time when a nation of colossal energies sought expression beyond that provided by the revival of historical styles. Modern architecture evolved as much in response to this demand as it did because of technological innovations. In his powerful buildings and, indeed, perhaps, in his own massive frame, Richardson epitomized this expression.

October, 1968   WILLIAM MORGAN
Newark, Delaware

To

THE PUPILS OF HENRY HOBSON RICHARDSON

this book is dedicated, as a testimony to the value of the assistance which they gave their master in his work and an expression of the belief that their own works will show, more convincingly than any words, the greatness of his qualities as an artist and a teacher.

M. G. VAN RENSSELAER.

9 WEST NINTH STREET, NEW YORK,
April 17, 1888.

CONTENTS.

———•———

APPENDIX.

LIST OF ILLUSTRATIONS.

FULL–PAGE PLATES.

ILLUSTRATIONS IN THE TEXT.

Beauty will not come at the call of a legislature, nor will it repeat in England or America its history in Greece. It will come, as always, unannounced, and spring up between the feet of brave and earnest men.

Emerson

HENRY HOBSON RICHARDSON.

CHAPTER I.

ANCESTRY AND EARLY LIFE.

HENRY HOBSON RICHARDSON was born at the Priestley Plantation in the Parish of St. James, Louisiana, on the 29th of September, 1838. His father was Henry Dickenson Richardson, a native of St. George's, Bermuda, and his mother was Catherine Caroline Priestley, a grand-daughter of that Dr. Priestley who was famous in his day for many things, but is now chiefly remembered as the discoverer of oxygen.

The first paternal ancestor of whom any record is preserved is James Richardson, who was born in London in 1695 and early in life emigrated to Bermuda. In 1722 he married Mary, daughter of Francis Dickenson of Port Royal, Bermuda, and his son Robert was born four years later. Robert married Mary Burchell, and their son, a second Robert, born in 1752, married for his third wife Honora Burrows. These were the parents of Henry Dickenson Richardson. His mother died at the moment of his birth, and his father while he was still a lad. When about sixteen years of age he removed to New Orleans, and entered into business as a cotton-merchant with the firm of Hobson & Company.

The maternal pedigree also begins in the seventeenth century, with Joseph Priestley, a "maker and dresser of woolen cloth" in Yorkshire.[1] His son Jonas married the daughter of Joseph Swift, a farmer, and their son, Joseph Priestley, afterwards the famous doctor, was born in 1733 at Fieldhead about six miles from Leeds. The story of his life is very interesting, but concerns us here only in so far as it explains the causes which brought him to America.

He was bred a Dissenter and entered the ministry. But even while studying at the theological academy he had shown that tendency toward independent thought which afterwards bore such conspicuous fruit. Even then, he tells us, he "saw reason to embrace what is generally called the heterodox side of things." As years went on he developed into a pronounced Socinian and an upholder of Necessitarian doctrines in philosophy; and as he always expressed each phase of his opinions with entire frankness — not to say impetuosity — of both speech and pen, he was constantly embroiled in theological battles which yearly grew more hot and bitter. His scientific investigations brought him a less thorny crown of fame.

[1] *Memoirs of Dr. Joseph Priestley to the Year 1795. Written by himself. With a continuation to the Time of his Decease, by his Son, Joseph Priestley; and Observations on his Writings by Thomas Cooper, President* Judge of the 5th District of Pennsylvania; and the Reverend William Christie. Northumberland: Printed by John Binns, 1806. (Issued also in London, 1805–1807.)

But as he also interested himself in social questions, and here too took his stand among the boldest Radicals of that excited day, political as well as religious hatred long raged against him, not only in the neighborhoods where he dwelt but throughout the length and breadth of England; and when in 1791 he boldly expressed his sympathy with the revolutionists of France, conservative passion could no longer contain itself. His house and laboratory in Birmingham were burned by a frantic mob, he was obliged to flee for his life, and even in London was compelled to hide for a time from his enemies.

A curious old aquatint, a copy of which is still in the possession of the Richardson family, shows the ruin to which his home had been reduced. One imagines that some sympathetic feeling must have prompted its publication, for a group of short-waisted ladies and long-coated gentlemen stand in the foreground and lift their hands as though in lamentation. But so little sympathy was shown by his countrymen at large that he soon shook English dust from his feet and in 1794 set sail for America, whither his three sons had preceded him.

We may be proud that the young republic was so much less bigoted and fearful than the mother-country that she gave him honorable reception. He was welcomed by addresses and deputations when he landed in New York, and might at once have established himself as Unitarian preacher and philosophic lecturer in either New York or Philadelphia. But before deciding what his new life should be, he went to Northumberland (a little town at the confluence of two branches of the Susquehanna River, about one hundred and thirty miles northeast of Philadelphia) to inspect a district where his eldest son and some other Englishmen were planning to establish an agricultural colony. He himself was never concerned in this land-scheme, which, indeed, was soon abandoned. But he was charmed by the beauty and apparent healthfulness of Northumberland, was more attracted by its promise of leisure and retirement than by the offers of public usefulness which the large cities held out to him, and soon decided to make it his permanent home. Hither he brought his books and his scientific instruments, and here, in a comfortable house to which was attached a good laboratory, he dwelt for the rest of his years, going, however, from time to time to Philadelphia to deliver courses of lectures on various philosophical themes. He studied, experimented, and wrote as diligently as he had done at home, and still argued with zeal on many matters of public interest. Not a few heated paper battles were the result, but they showed scarce a sign of that bitterness of personal invective which had characterized the opposition to his views in England. The nearest approach to persecution that he experienced in America was when certain political writings, in which he had criticised the course of the Federalist party, drew from John Adams the advice to speak no more on such topics "lest he get himself into trouble."

During his later years Dr. Priestley suffered much from disease and weakness, and he died at Northumberland in 1804 at the age of sixty-one. He had married in early life Mary, the daughter of Isaac Wilkinson, an iron-master living near Wrexham in Wales. She died in 1796, at the age of fifty-five, and lies buried beside her husband.

Their second son, William, from whom Richardson was descended, was born in Leeds. He was with his father at the time of the Birmingham outrage, fled to France to escape the after-claps of the popular storm, and became naturalized as a citizen of the new republic. But French air was likewise filled with storms, and what with Conservative intolerance on one side of the Channel and Radical excesses on the other, the Old World seemed to have no place where a quiet man might gain his livelihood by trade. An elder and a younger brother were already in America, and hither William Richardson came, too, a short time before his father's immigration. After his arrival he married Margaret Foulke, who was also of English birth, — a native of Northumberlandshire and probably of Birmingham. Her father, Joseph Foulke, was a gentleman of Scotch descent, and her mother belonged to that Chambers family which founded Chambersburg in Pennsylvania.

William Priestley remained but a short time with his father in Pennsylvania. About the year 1801 he removed to Louisiana, in the belief that the cultivation of sugar-cane would prove a profitable employment. Nor was he mistaken, for he soon owned large and flourishing plantations and amassed a fortune — very considerable in those days — of several hundred thousand dollars. His daughter, Catherine Caroline Priestley, was born at the Priestley Plantation, and, as has been told, married Henry Dickenson Richardson and became the mother of the architect. He was the eldest of a family of four, — the others being one brother, Mr. William Priestley Richardson who served with distinction in the Civil War as an officer of the Confederate army and who now lives in New Orleans, and two sisters who are married to Mr. John W. Labouisse and Mr. Henry Leverich of the same city. His father died at Philadelphia in 1854, and his mother subsequently married Mr. John D. Bein who had been the business partner of her late brother, Mr. William Priestley. Both Mr. and Mrs. Bein died some years ago.

The mothers of great men, even unto the third and fourth generation, have a proverbial interest for the biographer. Dr. Priestley's wife, according to his own testimony, was the faithful, intelligent, and courageous sharer of his troubled life, — " a woman of excellent understanding, much improved by reading, of great fortitude and strength of character, and of a temper in the highest degree affectionate and generous ; feeling strongly for others and little for herself. Also, greatly excelling in everything relating to household affairs, she entirely relieved me of all concern of that kind, which allowed me to give all my time to the prosecution of my studies and the other duties of my station." Of Margaret Foulke, William Priestley's wife, Mr. William Priestley Richardson writes : " My grandmother died in New Orleans, at the age, I believe, of eighty-five. I well remember her, and have often heard her spoken of as most accomplished in all that pertains to womanly virtue, and as having a constitution of mind, remarkable in her time, which enabled her to give personal attention, after the death of her husband, to all the important details of her business, — the management of large plantation interests, — and after the death of her son William to share in the control of the large hardware firm of Priestley & Bein to which he had belonged." And her daughter, Mrs. Richardson, by the same evidence, " inherited in the highest degree all her gentler qualities of heart and mind, and was truly a most devoted friend and mother."

Richardson's early life was passed chiefly in New Orleans, though the summer months and the winter vacations were spent at the plantation where he and his mother had been born. When not more than seven years of age he was sent to the public school then held in the basement of the Presbyterian Church on Lafayette Square. But he remained there only a few months. His systematic education began in a private school kept by Mr. George Blackman, and was there carried on until the autumn following his father's death. It had been intended that he should enter the army, and through Mr. Judah P. Benjamin, an intimate friend of his father's, the chance of a cadetship at West Point was secured. But an impediment in his speech rendered him unfit for military service, and after a year at the University of Louisiana he went to Cambridge, Mass., to prepare for Harvard with a private tutor.

Early in his school life he showed signs in which we can now read the budding talent of the architect. When about ten years old his love for drawing induced his father to place him, with pupils of much greater age, under the best master in New Orleans; and in mathematics he was exceptionally proficient from the very first. Both Mr. Blackman and Professor Sears, the head of the University of Louisiana, were accomplished mathematicians, and both delighted in his rapid progress and saw therein the prophecy of a distinguished future. When he first went to Cambridge he might easily have passed in mathematics into the Sophomore, or probably even into the Junior class. Backwardness in the classics, however, compelled further preparation, and he matriculated with the class of '59. At this time he was already a good French scholar; for though no French blood ran in his veins, he had been taught the language at home as well as in his school classes.

His childhood seems to have been of the happiest, and the memory of his companions shows him to us in a most attractive light. He was an eager, active, affectionate, generous, and merry boy, working well at school, and, whenever ambition prompted, easily excelling his fellows in all out-door sports and athletic exercises. Later he became a good horseman, and, as his father had been before him, an expert with the foils. From his father too, as well as from all the Priestleys, he inherited a great fondness for chess, and it is said that even blindfold he could successfully play several games at once. He loved music, and learned to play well on the flute; and, to quote his brother's words, " he was fond of ladies' society, and consequently always scrupulously neat and tasteful in his dress. This love of dress grew with him. His 'mock part' in college was 'Nothing to Wear,' from the fact that he had better clothes and more of them than any one man needed."

His college life was uneventful. He took and kept a fair standing in his class, but does not seem to have been an especially diligent student, or to have shown marked ability in any branch save mathematics. His proficiency in this branch all his classmates recollect; and all remember his social disposition and his great personal charm. " It is pleasant," says one who was a fellow-student, though not a classmate,[1] " to go back and recall the slender, companionable Southern lad, full of creole life and animation. . . . In recent years he was 'a good portly man and a corpulent, of a cheerful look, a pleasing eye, and a most noble carriage;'

[1] Charles Francis Adams, Jr.: Address delivered at Cambridge, Mass., on Commencement Day, June, 1886.

but in those early days . . . he was, like Falstaff at the same period of life, 'not an eagle's talon in the waist.'" He was then, indeed, a very handsome youth, above the medium height, slightly and gracefully built, with thick, curly dark hair, a warm complexion, very dark and brilliant hazel eyes, a rather thin long face, and finely-moulded features — the firmly compressed yet mobile and humorous mouth speaking both the energy and the gayety of his disposition. Handsome and distinguished in appearance, vivacious and sympathetic in manner, forcible and amusing in conversation, clever, ardent, and impressionable, — rich too, and, we are told, "generous to a fault," — it is no wonder that his college days should have been pleasant, or that they should have brought him many friends. It is a better proof that he had the power of winning true affection and of bestowing it in return, to find that the friends then made remained the friends of a life-time. Their love for "Fez," as they affectionately called him, and the interest they felt in his career, were never interrupted for a day, despite his long absence from America and the strain of that terrible conflict which severed so many of the ties that had bound together Americans of northern and of southern birth. They made him many generous offers of assistance during his time of poverty and struggle in Paris ; their welcome after six years of separation was as heartfelt as their god-speed had been ; and those who were his closest friends at college were still among his closest when he died.

His Alma Mater had no more loyal or grateful son than this one, born in a far-off State, whom the chances of later life brought back to dwell almost at her doors. He often spoke of all she had done for him, especially in the way of widening his life and enriching it with friends. No commission to work pleased him so much as a commission to work for her ; and if one chanced to cite Sever Hall as perhaps the most perfect of his structures, he was ready for her sake to delight in the verdict. And I think no social distinction which could have come to him in later life could have given him so much satisfaction as his membership in that very ancient and "exclusive" college club — The Porcellian — which admits only fifteen undergraduates at a time but keeps all whom it admits in close brotherhood ever after.

Richardson's intention on leaving the South had been to make civil engineering his profession. Neither his family nor his classmates remember just when he changed his mind, or just what led him to think of the architectural profession instead. Nor have I been able to discover any evidence in his own handwriting — all the letters he wrote home from Cambridge having been destroyed when his family left New Orleans before the arrival of the Union troops. A short time before his graduation he heard with pleasure that his step-father had resolved to send him to Europe to prosecute his architectural studies ; and as soon as his examinations were over he set sail with two of his classmates, spent the summer traveling in England, Scotland, and Ireland, and then settled down to his work in Paris.

While still at college he had engaged himself to Miss Julia Gorham Hayden, daughter of Dr. John Cole Hayden of Boston.

CHAPTER II.

LIFE IN PARIS.

VERY few of Richardson's letters from Paris have been preserved — only a single one addressed to an uncle in New Orleans, and a short series, covering a period of about four months, written to his future wife. Fortunately they chance to speak of significant days and things, and the memory of his friends helps us to complete at least an outline of the picture we should have liked to see fully painted by himself.

The letter to his uncle is dated November 23, 1860, more than a year later than his arrival in Europe, and conveys the news of his admission to the great Paris art-school.

"Last Tuesday I was admitted member of l'Ecole des Beaux Arts. No one knew I intended presenting myself. . . . I have no time to write you a detailed account of the examinations. Suffice it to say they lasted one month, were public, and carried on entirely in French. I was once sick and was obliged to present an unfinished design; but notwithstanding I entered well. One hundred and twenty presented themselves, sixty only were accepted, I being the eighteenth. I had the disadvantage of being a foreigner, — got confused at my mathematical examination, and that brought my average down."

Certainly this is a very good showing for one who passed his examinations in a foreign tongue, and who had had no preparatory instruction before leaving home except in mathematics. There is no record of any artistic study during his earlier years save such as is implied by the drawing-lessons of his childhood and by certain others followed, with how much diligence does not appear, during his college terms. It seems, however, that he had been far from realizing what such an examination would mean even as regarded mathematics, and had tried in vain to pass it immediately upon his arrival.

"My first recollection of Richardson," writes Mr. R. Phené Spiers, the distinguished English architect, who studied at the same time in Paris though in a different *atelier*, " was in September or October, 1859, when he presented himself for examination at the Ecole des Beaux Arts. He had come over about a month previous in the hope of being able to pass the examination straight off. Two *vive voce* examinations in algebra and geometry he managed to pass, but the stiff questions in descriptive geometry (the study of which he had only taken up about a month before) floored him, and he had to wait until 1860, when he entered the school."

The intervening months were passed in steady preparatory work.

"I remember him," writes an American friend,[1] " living in a sort of *pension* in

---

[1] Mr. Joseph Bradlee.

the Rue de Vaugirard, working hard at French, and getting himself up on the subjects for examination at the Ecole. . . . He was then receiving regular remittances of money from New Orleans which enabled him to live with ease. But his choice of a profession was a serious one, and he devoted himself to the study of it with the earnestness of a man for whom it was to be what the Germans call a 'bread-study.' In his second winter he left the Rue de Vaugirard, and took a pleasant apartment in the Rue de Luxembourg, on the other side of the river, now called the Rue Cambon. Here he lived until the Civil War at home interfered with his remittances of funds, — which first became irregular and finally wholly ceased, — and he was obliged to look for less expensive quarters. He accepted the situation cheerfully, and took a room in the not very attractive Rue Mazarin, which he occupied for some time during the latter part of his stay in Paris. The whole of his student life was passed, I believe, in the *atelier* of Monsieur André (Rue de l'Ecole des Beaux Arts), whom he liked personally, and for whose professional taste he always had great respect ; and with one or two of his French fellow-students there he formed lasting friendships. Richardson was an excellent companion, but though fond of pleasure and society and always ready for a dinner-party or a dancing-party, he never allowed these things to interfere with the serious performance of his work ; and many of his friends of that time will remember that he not infrequently returned late to his rooms after a party to finish the night in study ; or to his *atelier* when an exhibition of plans or drawings was in preparation. Cheerfulness and energy he seemed to have in unlimited quantity, both at this time and later, when illness and failing strength must have severely tried his patience. . . . Of course he made friends wherever he might be. In Paris they were among Frenchmen as well as Americans, Northerners and Southerners. He never, however, even in those hard times for him, appeared to have politics very much on his mind. At any rate there was no bitter partisan feeling, — indeed, bitterness was not in the man. He was quite absorbed in his profession, which he must have felt was, of necessity, to give him a career and means of support for himself and a probable family. His friends probably thought of him as 'Rich,' as he was familiarly called, without looking very closely as to whether he 'sympathized' with the North or the South. Many of them will have pleasant remembrances of him at the ——s' and ——s', and at the houses of others where Americans in Paris were in the habit of going five-and-twenty years ago. . . . For some of us who knew him in those earlier days in Paris, as a slender youth of promising talent, a good-tempered and amiable companion, it has been a delight to meet him from time to time during these recent years ; for we have always found him the same old 'Rich' we had known as younger men."

During the latter part of his stay in Paris, Richardson lived in the Rue du Bac with a fellow-student, Monsieur Adolphe Gerhardt, who afterwards gained a *prix de Rome*, and now holds a place among the eminent architects of France. For this friend Richardson always retained the warmest affection and gratitude, and for his talents the sincerest admiration. What have been Monsieur Gerhardt's feelings in return may best be read in his own words : —

AUTOGRAPH DRAWING BY H. H. RICHARDSON, 1859.

" . . . Coming to Paris in 1859, Richardson presented himself and was received at the *atelier* of Monsieur André, and a short time afterwards at the Ecole des Beaux Arts.[1] He enjoyed at this time pecuniary resources which permitted him to hope that he might pursue a long course of study free from all material cares. But ere long the outbreak of the War of Secession forced him to return to America. . . . At the beginning of the year 1862 he came back to Paris to resume with courage the course of his studies. Unfortunately a time soon arrived when these could no longer be his sole concern. His resources threatening to become exhausted, he husbanded them for a while as carefully as possible, but soon there remained for him no choice save to support himself by working as a draughtsman in architects' offices. From this moment there began for my poor friend an incessant battle between his aspirations and the needs of his existence. The chief thing for which he strove was not to be forced to leave the *atelier* of our dear master, Monsieur André. It was but at unduly long intervals that he could take part in the school competitions which lasted each for two full months. He was thus compelled to renounce the effort after successes to which he was well entitled to aspire; yet their absence left him with few regrets. The ambition which inspired him was of too healthy and too disinterested a sort for him to lay much stress upon the mere satisfaction of his *amour-propre*. The life of the *atelier*, — that existence of work and mutual encouragement, animated by much good-humor and gayety, — this it was that he had learned to love as heartily as any one of us. He followed with interest and ardor the labors of his comrades, regretting only that he was not always able to do as they were doing and take part in those peaceful conflicts which had as their arena the Salle des Compositions de Concours of the Ecole des Beaux Arts. Although long pieces of work were too often forbidden him, he yet 'kept his hand in' by making sketches for compositions to which he gave extraordinary charm and brilliancy. If the fact of his being a foreigner had not excluded him from the contests for the *prix de Rome*, he would have been among those most amply endowed for taking part in them.

" In addition to his architectural studies properly so called — which the necessities of his existence rendered somewhat desultory — our friend also sought instruction from a painter of talent, Monsieur Leperre, to whose studio he went two or three times a week. There, in the presence both of nature and of the antique, he completed an artistic education which he felt would be incomplete

[1] See Appendix II.

unless nourished by knowledge and intelligent appreciation of form and linear harmony as shown in their noblest and most elevated aspects. Our dear Richardson understood the importance of this principle from the outset ; and, in the application he made of it, showed that he had a true feeling for all artistic things, and that he realized one must aim high to attain to any excellence whatever. . . .

"I am sure that these years he passed in Paris, battling with adverse fortune, were not useless to his talent. Misfortune gave him a maturity of mind which is rarely exhibited by young men of his age. By the very stress of circumstances his thoughts were concentrated wholly on his work — he became an enthusiast, a devotee! I, who had the honor of being his friend and of sharing his life for more than two years, never had the chance to note any faltering, any feebleness in his valiant soul, — neither cowardly regrets nor unwholesome ambitions. In his heart he kept always intact and fresh a love for his art, a reverence for her who was to be his life's companion, and a pride in his fatherland." [1]

Mr. Spiers also speaks of the benefit it was to Richardson to be forced to struggle as he did : —

". . . All day working in an office . . . and every evening in his *atelier*, he managed to pursue his studies as before ; and probably by this accident were laid the foundations of his future career. The practical work of which he acquired a knowledge in the working-office and on the works is, I may say, never sought for by those who intend to practice in other countries, and who go to Paris to learn the art only and the theory of construction. . . ."

When, as Monsieur Gerhardt has told us, Richardson came to America in 1862, he at first thought of remaining in Boston and beginning the practice of his profession. He tried to find work, but the only definite opening that seems to have presented itself was with an architect of some standing who agreed to employ him if he would not put out his sign or accept any work in his own name. Such an offer would have seemed satisfactory to most young men in Richardson's position, but it by no means fell in with his desires. Then he thought seriously of going South, for his sympathies were naturally with his own people, although before the actual outbreak of the war he had felt and spoken strongly against secession. His Boston friends, however, vigorously opposed a step which would mean almost certain ruin to his career. Their efforts to induce him to take the oath of allegiance were in vain ; but he promised not to enter an insurrectionary State without their knowledge, and finally consented to go back to Paris and resume his studies.

The few letters which remain from the very many written to Miss Hayden during his student life, date from the months immediately following his return to

---

[1] This letter, together with those from Mr. Bradlee and Mr. Phené Spiers, and several others which I shall hereafter have occasion to quote, was written for publication at the request of the editors of *The American Architect and Building News*, when they contemplated making one number of their paper a special memorial of Mr. Richardson. With the greatest courtesy they abandoned their project upon learning that this book was in preparation, and permitted me to use the materials which they had been at the trouble of gathering.

Paris. The passages I am permitted to quote from them show how definitely his mind was now made up to complete his education, but do not half reveal how bitter was the struggle this resolution cost him.

March 13, 1862.

" . . . At last in Paris — it's a good old city, but on arriving yesterday morning I had mingled feelings of joy and sorrow. I went to my *atelier;* the fellows were delighted to see me, but Monsieur André is not well and I did not see him. . . .

March 27.

" . . . I think Paris a dangerous place to send a young man. Paris is to a man what college is to a boy. I mean as regards life. I never shall cease to thank Heaven for my short trip to Boston. . . . It gave me an opportunity of comparing side by side the habits, customs, lives, of the French and Anglo-Saxons. Had I remained longer in France I fear I should have been prejudiced. My feelings and ideas of French life are different from what they ever were before. I prefer our old-fashioned ways and ideas by far. . . . I have discussed the self-same topic at least a dozen times since my return, and have always taken up the cudgel for my own country. I mean, as a matter of course, from a social point of view. Politics I wash my hands of, externally at least. . . .

April 3.

" . . . Paris has no charms for me except my studies. My visit to you, and I thank Heaven for it, put an end to those it might have had. . . . I am now working at l'Ecole des Beaux Arts, and will continue to till I am obliged to work for money, for I gain more knowledge. . . .

April 10.

" . . . I am very, very busy, working on a Corps Législatif for exhibition. I am at the *atelier* every day till six P. M. (unless called off by business). I return at eight P. M. and remain till eleven P. M. That is my regular day's work. No one can say that I waste my time. . . . Last Friday I was at the *atelier* all night working for another man. I left the work at eight o'clock Saturday morning. The fall *may* bring me home, but I doubt it strongly. . . . Rest assured that no one wishes my return to Boston more sincerely than I. There is no use looking on the dark side. I have enough to struggle against without borrowing trouble. One of these days I may have my pleasures, at least I hope so — but as the French say, *toujours espérer, c'est désespérer.* . . .

April 17.

" . . . I am very busily engaged at present. I never leave the studio before eleven P. M., except Sundays, or when accidentally called off as last Tuesday, when I dined with —— and —— [friends from Boston], and went to the theatre in the evening. I see Miss —— every week, otherwise I go out not at all. Study and society are incompatible. . . . I see that operations have been commenced against New Orleans. I feel nervous and anxious to hear more. My poor mother and sisters — if I thought I could in any way aid them by being there, I would go to-morrow. You ask me what effect the capture of New Orleans would have on me. I don't know, but it would be folly to return immediately, a mere waste of time and money to come to Paris and stay but a few months. . . . I have given up hopes of receiving great aid from anything I may have in New Orleans. I am young, and I hope man enough to make my own way, and any stay I may make in Europe, feel assured, will be with the view of making both happier in the end. I want very much to go to Italy, and I intend to do it. . . . As that is a study I can undertake as well married as single, I may come home first. . . . If it is impossible for me to do it married, know that it is essential I go single. Neither you nor I will ever regret the time I pass perfecting myself in my studies. The more I study the nobler my profession becomes. . . .

April 25.

" . . . I hardly have time to take my meals. I am just waking up to the value of time, and, feeling I may be called away at any moment, I try to make the most of my days. But if I tell you in confidence I am working very hard . . . don't tell any one, not even your family. For two reasons: First, coming from you is the same as coming from myself, and amounts to self-praise. Second, there is no use in it, for if my work does me any good, the world will find it out of itself. . . . Since I last wrote I have done nothing but what I did the week before. . . . Last night I came home to write you as usual. I sat down in my easy-chair, took up my pencil and began to compose, meaning to pass half an hour or so. One of my candles burned out. I got up to get another, when, turning to the window, I saw the twilight. I looked at my watch — it was nearly five o'clock in the morning! . . . I have been for the last two days, and was last night, trying to compose a palace for the governor of Algiers and residence for the emperor — that is, besides my regular work, which is a Corps Législatif. The more I see and know of architecture, the more majesty the art gains. Oh, if I had begun at nineteen to study it! To Athens and Rome I must go, *coûte que coûte.*

May 1.

" . . . I am not very well nor have I been for a week past. I'm afraid it is sitting up too late. I can always work better at night. . . . My mind is always more active after eleven or twelve o'clock than at any other time. . . . I have no news whatever to write. My life is monotony itself, — to-day is as yesterday and to-morrow will be as to-day. In fact I live the life of a recluse and attempt that of a philosopher. . . . I can't say how long I will remain in Europe. It depends on various things . . . and you would prefer to have me remain a few months longer in Europe than return to America a second-rate architect. Our poor country is overrun with them now. I never will practice till I feel I can at least do my art justice. . . .

May 16.

" . . . New Orleans is taken — governed by strangers. . . . What a position to be placed in! My hands are tied, in one sense, from the many obligations under which I hold myself towards my friends in Boston; and there's not one of them for whom I would not personally undergo the greatest sacrifices. For their kindness I owe an everlasting debt. I have in vain reasoned about the right and wrong. . . . How I have suffered and do suffer, no one can ever know. To remain in Europe I think my best plan, — in fact I *must*. But I burned with shame when I read the capture of my city and I in Paris. What is to be the end I do not see. I received a letter from mother in which she begs me to remain where I am. . . .

May 23.

" . . . I intend studying my profession in such a manner as to make my success a surety and not a chance. We can then go anywhere in the beginning where good opportunities offer themselves. . . . I have written to Mr. —— in Liverpool as to money matters; if he holds money from my family, directly or indirectly, I shall accept it. If not, I shall immediately begin to support myself. It will come very hard to me, — not on account of the comforts I shall be in need of, but on account of my profession. Naturally, when I support myself I am employed to do things I am already versed in, whereas at l'Ecole des Beaux Arts, I am daily advancing in my studies, and every day I find new beauties in a profession which I already place at the head of all the Fine Arts. Therefore do not be surprised at my determination to avoid employment as long as I can. It suffices me to know that I can, when called upon, support myself — minus the luxuries. . . .

May 29.

" . . . I have taken a decided step. I have given up all hope of aid from home. I begin next week, or as soon as possible, to work for my living. . . . How I have suffered from it you will never know, for you know not how I love my art. . . . From this moment I am dependent on myself and on myself alone. Where or when I shall get employment I can't say. I trust it will be soon. I am going to attempt to support myself and carry on my studies at the same time; but whether I can do it or not is to be proved. But continue my studies I *must*, — there's no two ways about it. . . . How many are there worse off than I am! If I persevere I must succeed in the end, and my profession will be much dearer to me from the very pain it has caused me. . . . Let us hope for brighter days — they *must come*. It *seems* hard to me, but how many have done it before me. . . . I must stop, — it is now past one o'clock and I get up at seven. . . . I must come to the right side some time. " It's a long road that has no turning." I don't care about the want of money, but the time taken from my studies I regret. . . .

June 18.

" . . . You say again I cannot return to Boston. I can after the war, and it is quite possible that I will live there. I don't say it is probable, but it may happen. . . . I shall live where I can practice most profitably my profession, *wherever* it may be, provided there are no serious objections for your sake. . . . Mother says ' you must not think of returning home until peace is declared.'

July 4.

" . . . Yesterday and day before I had sketches at the school — twelve hours each ; in two days I worked twenty-four hours. Last night I left the school at nine P. M., came home, dressed myself, and went to dine at ten P. M. . . .

July 18.

" . . . I am now engaged in studying a Hospice des Incurables pour Hommes et Femmes.[1] It is quite a monument, to contain 2,000 persons, — invalids, a large church, nuns and nunnery, — in fact, a hospital of first importance, the total cost being two millions of dollars. Monsieur Labrouste has put into my hands the correspondence he had with the government, and told me to study it as I thought best. I rarely see him. I work at his house, but in a room entirely to myself — private. . . . My office hours are from between eight and nine till six. I am entirely alone, never see a person unless I go into Monsieur Labrouste's room to speak to him. . . . I come home at six, dress, dine, and in the evening either go to the studio, read in my room, or make visits. My habit is to study in the evening, visiting the exception, though lately I have been out a great deal. I gain between two hundred and three hundred francs a month. I did not ask for more. . . . Since I have been working I have felt more like myself than I have for a year. Although my troubles are just as great I feel happier. . . . Recollect I never studied architecture because it was a lucrative profession. . . .

August 6.

" . . . Why look upon the dark side ? . . . The day will come, and I trust it is not far distant, when talking of our misfortunes will only make our present happiness so much the greater. . . . The world owes us a living and our share of happiness. . . . Of one thing feel certain — the more we yield to pressure, the harder will be our lot. Just at present it does not look very bright, but it only calls for a little more courage and it will look less dark. . . .

August 29.

" . . . I am busy working on the hospital. I rise before eight, take a cup of coffee in my room, go to my office and remain there till half past five or six P. M. I then go to my room and dress for dinner. I dine about seven P. M. (for thirty-five cents). After my dinner I go to my room, smoke, and think . . . until nearly nine. Then to my studio until eleven P. M. Sometimes in the evenings — rarely — I make calls. I spend hardly anything. . . . What weighs most heavily on me is that I have not more time to carry on my studies. I ought to consider myself fortunate as it is; but man is never satisfied. . . . Economy is my hue and cry just now. I breakfast for twenty-five cents, dine for thirty-five, and pay fifty francs (ten dollars) a month for my room. Otherwise I spend very little. I *never* go to any place of amusement. . . ."

[1] It should be understood that the designing of this hospital was not a school task like the essays previously referred to, but a practical piece of work, undertaken by Richardson for self-support, in the office of one of the chief government architects of the day.

CHAPTER III.

LIFE IN PARIS AND RETURN TO AMERICA.

ENOUGH has been told in the foregoing chapter to prove that the trials of Richardson's student years were great, their privations manifold, and their outlook dark. But it would need a recital of facts and feelings too personal for these pages to show the full extent of the burden laid upon him, or of the courage with which he bore its weight. The war distressed him deeply from day to day, and so clouded the future that even his hopeful eye could see the opening of no definite professional path. As the many months went by, habit seems not to have inured him to the separation from those whom he held dear, but to have made it ever harder to support. The unfaltering vigor with which, in spite of all obstacles and discouragements, he pursued his studies is worthy of deep admiration. Only those who have tried to gain at the same time an education and a livelihood can understand how great must have been the temptation to think his training complete enough and to turn his whole thought to self-support; all the greater, too, by reason of his early wealth, and his naturally lavish and self-indulgent disposition. It must indeed have been, as Monsieur Gerhardt says, a " valiant soul " which could so long sustain so complicated a struggle, and a soul inspired by a true reverence for that art which can but too easily be turned into a mere money-making industry. And ability as well as energy and high courage must have been shown by Richardson at this time. I remember his saying that (at all events for a certain period) he worked half his days at getting his education and only half at earning his living. Certainly this implies ability, when one recollects that he was a foreigner with no friends except those whom he had made for himself, with no recommendation except his own talents, living in a city where the artistic professions are always overcrowded, and where, in the architectural profession especially, work that can find a market must be distinctly good. It was the influence of his *patron* that got him his first position in a government office. But no *patron* would have been likely to recommend an inefficient man to one of those establishments which demand and get the very best service the country has to give; and no recommendation unsupported by the outcome of practical tests would have advanced him to such work as he soon secured. At one time he acted under Hittorf in superintending the construction of various railroad stations; and he has himself told of the tasks to which he was put by Labrouste — tasks which related to work of a very important and difficult kind, and which were not mechanical or merely executive, but to a great degree independent and creative.

In the Paris of to-day there is a large colony of American artists, — painters, sculptors, architects, studying or practicing their crafts, — which is recognized as an important and honored factor in local artistic life. Its mere existence serves to recommend each new-comer and to give him a good chance to show what may in him lie, while its individual members are ready to aid him with counsel and example, and with a brotherly hand in days of need. But American students were very rare in the Paris of Richardson's day. Then, as now, the government schools were open to all comers, but few aspirants in any branch had yet crossed the Atlantic to take advantage of their hospitality. Mr. Richard M. Hunt had graduated with distinction some years before from the Ecole des Beaux Arts, and had afterwards been employed on government work as important as the construction of the new Louvre. But, so far as can be learned, his was the only American name that had preceded Richardson's on the roll of the Architectural Section, and only one or two others were added while Richardson's remained. Richardson worked and lived as an isolated foreigner; or, one may more truly say, as a Frenchman among Frenchmen — for warm affection and brotherly help soon came to him in as full a measure as though his friends had been his fellow-countrymen. Many delightful letters which they wrote him (of too purely personal a sort to call for insertion here) show the reflex of his frank, ardent, and attractive personality. Then, as in all later years, men wrote to Richardson in a strain which proves a much warmer sort of attachment than commonly exists between man and man after maturity has come.

When his lot had so changed that the memory of this past time of trial only made, as he had foretold, his "present happiness seem greater," it was both amusing and inspiring to hear Richardson's own account of it — vivid, enthusiastic, humorous, yet showing that undercurrent of serious thought and profound feeling which always revealed itself in all talks that touched upon his art or the ambitions of his life. One realized then that this time had had its bright as well as its shadowed side even while it passed. One felt the truth of his friend Gerhardt's impression — that the energy of his nature had been sufficient not only to carry him through his struggles, but to make even the act of struggling a stimulus and a pleasure. Many were his tales of the curious, dramatic, or pathetic incidents of the motley life of the Latin Quarter. Many were his recollections of the wild gayety of his friends when some difficult task, left for completion to last hurried hours of all-night work, had been finished and displayed, and the *atelier* — through some one of its members in whose success all the others felt they had a right to share — had triumphed over rival studios in a general *concours* of the School.

Most picturesque of all was his account of that great, and now historic, student "strike" which occurred when Viollet-le-Duc had been appointed lecturer in opposition to all the traditions and to the very decided protests of the School. The lecture-room was packed when the famous mediævalist first appeared, but with an audience noisily determined not to listen to so much as his first word. And when he had been driven discomfited from the platform, his adversaries, joined by a swarm of sympathizing students of all sorts, defiantly paraded the *quais* till the police laid violent hands upon them. Of course Richardson's sympathies were with the insurgents. But as a foreigner he felt himself a guest of the government and no sharer in the right of the *citoyen* to appeal from its decisions. This feeling was strong enough to hold him aloof from the demonstration in the School, but not from the street parade. Among those captured by the police, he was locked up for official examination on the following day. But being dignified to the eye, as he would explain, " by good clothes from Poole's," he was put in a private cell with only a single companion — a strange-looking, long-haired gentleman of enchanting conversational powers. Half the night had passed merrily between them when the door was thrown open and a dignitary in evening dress appeared, blazing with stars and ribbons. This proved to be Nieuwerkerke, the offending and now in his turn offended Minister of Fine Arts ; and Richardson's companion, in answer to whose appeal the great man had come, proved to be Théophile Gautier. Of course Richardson at once began impetuously to plead for his own release ; and of course his frank and charming eloquence won the day. It all sounds tame enough as here recited, but was immensely amusing when told in his graphic pantomime and in those rapid words which were emphasized into greater piquancy by his slightly stammering tongue. The vivacious delight with which he described how he left the jail in triumph between the be-starred and be-ribboned official and the famous poet, was matched by the conscientious earnestness with which he explained how it was not against Viollet-le-Duc himself that the students had protested, but against a government which in his appointing had " dared to try to coerce the School," and the boyish zest with which he exulted in the School's final winning of its righteous battle.

From his step-father's letter already referred to, written in February, 1859, it appears that Richardson was expected to stay but some six or eight months in London or Paris, and then return to study and practice his profession in New Orleans. But his sojourn abroad was prolonged for six years and a half. It was not until October, 1865, when the war was well over and business affairs had begun to be straightened out, that he finally set sail for home. And then it was not to New Orleans that he went. He never even visited his native town again, although I have heard him speak of a constant wish to do so. New York was chosen as the best place in which to try his fortune, and the commissions which afterwards marked out his life came exclusively from the Northern States.

Advice of many sorts had been offered him during his last year in Paris. His French friends begged him to cast in his lot with theirs — to become naturalized as a Frenchman and then try for that *prix de Rome* to which he had already every other title to aspire, or at least to take advantage of the assured position which he had earned by his satisfactory service under government. His Boston friends urged — indeed almost dictated as a course about which there could be no question — that he should come back to them.[1] His family wrote that peace would mean renewed prosperity for New Orleans and a good opening for his talent there. And a more singular suggestion more than once seriously made

---

[1] One of them writes, just after the close of the war, that Boston is in truth full of young men out of work and needing it badly, but that those who earnestly seek will no doubt eventually find it, and that meanwhile Richardson is invited to return and become a member of a proposed club, " carefully selected, to be called the *Hors d'Œuvres.*"

to him by Southern correspondents was that he might secure a great future by settling in Mexico. This was at the time when Maximilian's throne seemed to give some promise of stability.

All these suggestions (excepting the last named) Richardson considered and discussed in his letters. But the ties which bound him to the Northern States were strongest; and here too, he wisely felt, lay at just that time his richest chances of professional success. There are no letters, however, and no distinct memories to prove just what reasons led him to New York instead of to Boston, where he was so much more at home.

Immediately after his return he seems to have entered into some kind of a partnership with a builder in Brooklyn named Roberts; but little can be learned about this association, and he soon broke away from it, took an office in New York, and looked about for independent work. He was wholly without resources for the future; — even the fine library he had gathered during his college life and the first months of his stay in Paris had been already sold. He made no complaints, however, and seldom allowed despondency to appear in his manner. No false pride stood in the way of his accepting any employment, however humble — once he even went to Tiffany & Co. and offered himself, apparently without success, as a designer of gas-fixtures; yet no false modesty led him to hide his belief that he had the ability which would bring success in his own high profession could he but get "one chance to show what he could do."

"Let me describe him," writes a lady who befriended him at this time when he was boarding in Brooklyn,[1] "exactly as I recall to-day his looks. . . . He was of good height, broad-shouldered, full-chested, dark complexion, brown eyes, dark hair parted in the centre, and had the look of a man in perfect health and with much physical vigor. He wore his clothes, which fitted him well, with an indescribable air of ease . . . like one who had dressed himself properly in his room and thought no more about it afterwards than he did about the color of his hair or the shape of his head. . . . His cravats had a careless ease. . . . His shoes were thick, broad-soled, and looked more as if made in England than in France. . . .

"We had been boarding a month or two at the same house when I had an opportunity to buy a pretty little house and . . . decided to go to housekeeping. Mr. Richardson . . . came into my room and said, 'Mrs. P., I want you to take me as a boarder. . . . All I want for breakfast is hash, with the addition of a cup of coffee so strong that you can never wash the cup white after using.' . . .

"He occupied a small back parlor, quiet and retired. Here he brought his library, and here he spent many hours of patient study. . . . After a few weeks he came to me and said, 'I have dissolved my partnership, I stand alone in the world without the means to pay my way.' There was a proud humility in his manner which amused and interested me. 'Do not be troubled,' I said, 'something favorable will turn up after a while. Stay on with us.' . . . I knew he was in perplexity, but I failed at the time to fathom the undercurrent of de-

[1] Letter in *Boston Evening Transcript*, October 8, 1886.

spondency which troubled his life. . . . He was going to the Century Club one evening, and as he passed out of his room he said, 'Look at me. I wear a suit made by Poole, of London, which a nobleman might be pleased to wear, and — and — and I have n't a dollar to my name.' He said this so cheerfully, with that same proud humility to which I have referred, that even then I did not realize his despondency. It was a dark hour to him. . . . Not far from this time came the sad news of his mother's death. At once — he could hardly wait for the next train — he must go for sympathy to the one who held the place in his heart next his mother. There was a childlike simplicity about this man which he may have hidden as he came more in contact with the world and his life was filled with work and care ; but it was in his nature. . . .

"At last he disappeared for a day or two. On his return he said that . . . he was to be the architect of a new church in Springfield, Mass. He went to work with great interest, though he had not been idle during his waiting time. . . . One thing is certain, if 'the value of any work of art is exactly in the ratio of the quantity of humanity put into it,' then Mr. Richardson's work was good, for he put his soul into it. He believed in 'bold, rich, living architecture,' and in good work or none. . . . He did not like that the architect should be fettered by lack of money in the client. In his view the best use of money is to spend it in architecture to which posterity may point with pride. . . ."

It was in the month of November, 1866, after he had been more than a year at home, that Richardson got that first commission to which reference has just been made. When the competition for a large Unitarian church to be built in Springfield was opened, a former classmate, Mr. J. A. Rumrill, obtained for him permission to send in his designs with those of several well-known architects. Much opposition was made by more than one member of the building-committee to the idea of intrusting so important a piece of work to an untried man — to a man who had had no independent practice and no especial training in the kind of design required, and whose knowledge of practical matters in America must evidently be very small. Nevertheless the intrinsic merits of his project carried the day. He had come himself to Springfield in his impatience to learn the committee's decision and was awaiting it in an outer room. When it was told him he burst into tears and exclaimed, " That is all I wanted — *a chance.*"

And a chance was all he needed. Almost at once he received another important commission in Springfield, and within the year he was successful in a competition for an Episcopal church at West Medford, near Boston, and could feel himself fairly launched in professional life.

On the strength of his very first piece of work he married Miss Hayden, — in January, 1867, — and established his home at Clifton, Staten Island.

CHAPTER IV.

PROFESSIONAL LIFE.

RICHARDSON'S first place of business was in Trinity Building, on Broadway, where he was permitted to occupy a room in the offices of Mr. Emlin J. Littell, architect. Here he worked for some eighteen months upon the commissions for his first three buildings, — the Church of the Unity and the Boston & Albany Railroad offices in Springfield, and Grace Church at West Medford, Massachusetts.

Just two years after his return to America (October 1, 1867), he entered into partnership with Mr. Charles Gambrill, an architect of well-established reputation who seems to have known and befriended him during the foregoing months. The firm of Gambrill & Post, of which the second member had been Mr. George B. Post, was dissolved at this time, and that of Gambrill & Richardson was immediately formed, Richardson removing to his partner's offices at No. 6 Hanover Street. Later on the firm was housed at No. 57 Broadway, a building which, in the new guise given it by Messrs. Babb, Cook & Willard, is still the professional home of many architects.

This partnership lasted for eleven years, — until October, 1878, soon after which time Mr. Gambrill died. Many of Richardson's works therefore, and some of great importance, including Trinity Church in Boston, were designed under the firm name.[1] But as works of art they were not in any true sense the products of associated labor. The partnership was even more exclusively of a business nature than those which usually bind architects together, and each member executed his own tasks in his own individual way. There is no question that Richardson owed a great and constantly recurring debt to the business experience and practical knowledge of Mr. Gambrill. But his artistic independence is clearly acknowledged by Mr. Gambrill himself in letters which still exist, was very soon unmistakably manifest in his productions, and was generally understood at the time by those who knew them both. Not merely when Trinity Church was commissioned but at an even earlier period, men thought and spoke of Richardson as an independently creative artist, and were fully justified in so speaking by all laws except those of the narrowest professional etiquette.

It is not proposed to describe any of his works in this chapter, — they will be better considered by themselves when the main facts of his life have been told, — and only those need be even mentioned which conspicuously influenced that life by their success.

The first which thus claims attention is the Brattle Square Church in Boston,

---

[1] See List of Works, Appendix I.

the commission for which was gained in competition in July, 1870 — two years after the formation of the partnership. No building that had been erected in Boston within the memory of younger generations had compelled half the notice which this excited, even before its elaborate sculptured decorations were in place ; and the general admiration for it was great enough to justify the selection of its designer as one of those who should compete for the proposed new church for Trinity parish.

When the invitation to do this was before him, Richardson knew that a critical moment in his career had come. " The chance " for which he had longed in order that he might show himself an architect had been given him in the Springfield church, and had been so well used that now, at thirty-four years of age, after only five years of practice, he was given a chance to show whether or not he was a great architect. Trinity was to be a church of unusual size and costliness, and was sure to be exceptionally conspicuous by reason of the isolation and dignity of its site, and, I may add, the wide fame of its pastor ; and in competing for it, Richardson was to measure himself against a number of the most distinguished architects of the country. While preparing his designs he knew that he was dealing with the signal opportunity of his life ; and when they had been chosen he knew that he had gained a marked professional victory and a most fortunate opening for full and decided self-expression.

It was a great test, but it resulted in a triumph which seemed greater and greater as actual construction progressed. Trinity grew to be a far finer building than the designs had promised, and it did more for Richardson than even he himself could have hoped. Not only was it a turning-point in his outer professional career, — it is also the most conspicuous mile-stone which marks the course of his inner artistic development. The practice given by so large and ornate a group of buildings was of inestimable advantage at this stage in his life. Their general success confirmed his belief in the great possibilities and the wide serviceableness of Romanesque forms, while their defects as well as beauties helped to settle into a far clearer scheme his conception of the way in which these forms should be used. When he began Trinity all his work had been merely tentative, and it was itself but a great and bold experiment. When he finished it he was already erecting other buildings which are mature and characteristic expressions of his power. When he began it he was a very promising architect who had attracted a greater measure of popular attention than usually falls to the share of such an one in our day and land. When he finished it he was to his countrymen at large the best known and most interesting figure in the profession. While he was still in Paris his brother had written him that " he gave him five years to stand at the head of his profession." The prophecy was bold, but was almost literally fulfilled.

The commission for Trinity was received in July, 1872, and the completed and decorated structure was consecrated on the 9th of February, 1877. Meanwhile another most important piece of work of a very different sort had been undertaken. In 1876 the Legislature of the State of New York confided to Richardson, in company with Mr. Leopold Eidlitz, architect, and Mr. Frederick Law Olmsted, landscape architect, the responsible, difficult, and in many ways ungrateful task of completing the State Capitol at Albany. Much of Richardson's time was given to this task, especially during the next succeeding years, but it was far from being finished when he died.

The next commissions he received were for public library buildings in the towns of Woburn and North Easton, in eastern Massachusetts, — the one in March and the other in September, 1877. With these closes the list of works to which the firm name of Gambrill & Richardson was attached. Trinity Church and other New England structures gradually claimed so large a portion of Richardson's time that in the spring of 1874 he removed his family from Staten Island to Brookline, four miles from Boston; and his practice grew gradually more and more independent — as is shown, for example, by the Albany commission, which was given to himself individually and not to his firm. Thus the ties of partnership had so relaxed that when they were severed in October, 1878, no public announcement of the fact was made. Richardson's offices were now also removed to Brookline and accommodated under the same roof with his home; and here, amid singularly advantageous and congenial surroundings, he lived and worked during the eight years that remained to him.

The commission to build Sever Hall for Harvard College was the first that he received after the dissolution of his partnership. But it is not needful in this place to follow farther the long list of his works. Their number is not remarkable if, in comparing it with the number which fell to the lot of other prominent architects during the same term of years, one counts building against building without regard to relative importance. But it seems very great if one considers the character of Richardson's structures, — if one notes how many are of the monumental class, and notes, too, how pronounced is that diversity which meant at almost every step a new problem with new difficulties of its own. Town work and rural work; municipal buildings, libraries, and churches; railroad stations and dwellings; wholesale warehouses and retail stores; bridges, monuments, fountains, armories, succeed each other beneath his busy hand. And the variety which the list reveals has a double interest and significance, — as showing, first, that Richardson delighted to embrace every kind of opportunity, whether great or small; and secondly, that the public had begun to feel that small architectural opportunities, as well as great ones, require the service of the ablest minds.

The most singular fact to be noted with regard to the work of Richardson's latter years is that ecclesiastic commissions were so few. First the Springfield church, then the Brattle Square Church, and then and above all Trinity — these had been the three buildings to make his name and to draw popular attention to his art. Yet after the commission for Trinity was received he built but two churches, and these were by no means of the first importance.

This fact, however, cannot be counted a misfortune either for himself or for the public. His natural bent was much more towards secular than towards ecclesiastical architecture. He was born a creator not a student, an innovator not an antiquary. A feeling for the vital serviceableness of his art was very strong within him, and therefore he cared more to work on new than on traditional lines. What he loved best was the freshest problem. What he most rejoiced in was to give true yet beautiful expression to those needs which were wholly modern in their genesis and had hitherto been overlooked by art. No architect so endowed as to be very strongly attracted by ecclesiastical work would have been likely to say what I once heard Richardson say: "The things I want most to design are a grain-elevator and the interior of a great river-steamboat."

Once indeed in his later years he put on paper his conception of what a church of the most monumental kind should be. The most elaborate and most scholarly designing he ever did is shown in the splendid series of competition-drawings for the Protestant cathedral at Albany. Nowhere else are his purely æsthetic aspirations set forth upon so noble and complete a scale, or with such richness of detail and accessory decoration. But when the terms of the competition are examined and these drawings are studied by their light, it seems certain that he could have had no sober expectation of being allowed to build in any near accordance with his submitted scheme.

The truth seems to be that when once this scheme had taken hold of Richardson's imagination he threw himself into it with uncalculating ardor and developed it for the mere pleasure of the task. To a true artist there is no delight so great as to find or fancy himself for once amid ideal conditions — free to do his best and greatest, unfettered and unquestioned, with no laws or limits to respect save those prescribed by art itself and the farthest reach of his own powers. It would be difficult to say just how definitely Richardson recognized, in the enthusiasm of the moment, that these conditions were in this case fancied and not found. At all events, though he was deeply chagrined and disappointed when the commission was denied him, he soon realized that to have been kept from building his cathedral was a positive piece of good fortune. "It would have been delightful work," he often said, " but I had not the time to spare for it — there is so much other work to do and of so much more necessary kinds. Fifteen years of labor on a cathedral was not the thing I should have hoped for."

Nor would it have been the best thing for his fellow-countrymen had the last and strongest years of Richardson's life been chiefly occupied in such a task. Churches of certain sorts are needed to-day, of course, as well as secular structures; and they also need the exercise of the best creative power — need to be adapted and not copied from the examples of some elder time. To build a church like Trinity — large but not excessively large, and planned to meet the actual needs of a modern Protestant congregation, — to build one like that Baptist church at Newton, Mass., which he finished but shortly before his death — modest in size and planned for a modern congregation with special ritual needs, — these were indeed worthy tasks; for they were tasks which required for their right fulfillment fresh study of fundamental problems as well as artistic taste and knowledge, and which, if rightly fulfilled, would be of helpful influence in many a future case. But it is a question whether our modern Protestant America really needs a vast and ornate cathedral church planned on mediæval lines. And it is certain that even if Richardson had built one as beautiful as his designs foreshadow, it would have been of small practical aid towards the general development of American art. It would have been a far more superb monument to the æsthetic side of his power than anything he constructed. But it would not have been such a monument to the practical usefulness of that power, or such a prophecy of the progress of our architecture as a genuinely vital art, as are the municipal and commercial structures upon which instead the efforts of his later years were spent. No cathedral, however magnificent in scheme or perfect in detail, would be worth so much to us as the Pittsburgh Court-house or the great simple Field Building in Chicago; and we should be unwilling to take it in exchange for that series of modest railroad stations which has done so much to lift the stigma of obligatory ugliness from one of the most important architectural novelties of our time.

In Richardson's own estimation the Pittsburgh building was the great work of his life — the most interesting and important as a problem and the most entirely successful in result; and he was especially proud of the chance to build it as the invitation to compete had come from so distant a spot and had been prompted by the sight of his works alone and not by a personal acquaintance of any member of the committee with himself. He knew his life might be very short and was almost feverishly anxious to see the Court-house complete before he died. "Let me but have time to finish Pittsburgh," he often exclaimed, "and I should be content without another day."

He had been gifted with a strong constitution and a fine physique. But while in Paris he met with a serious accident from the painful results of which he never recovered, and for years before his death he suffered from a dangerous chronic disease that called for constant precautions. Often he was kept for many days at home by its attacks or actually confined to his bed; and he gradually grew so very stout that his weight alone might have been thought an almost prohibitive obstacle to bodily exertion. Yet in spite of everything he seemed much the most active and energetic, much the most alive of all the men one knew.

An intense, immense vitality, physical as well as mental and emotional, was his most distinctive characteristic. Every one had been told that his life was in danger, but no one could believe it in his presence, for there seemed strength enough in him to do the work of six and life enough to last out three times our three-score years and ten. Every one knew he suffered greatly, but few could realize the fact, his patience was so unfailing, his spirits so high, his delight in life so peculiarly apparent. No man ever asked less for pity or seemingly pitied himself less than this man who, after a long period of struggle, was now on the top wave of success; who was leading just the life amid just the surroundings which he would have chosen; who had done so much but knew so well he could do so much more and better; who felt and confessed a childlike pleasure as well as a manly pride in his great talent and his noble opportunity — and was yet aware that all might be at an end for him to-morrow. He bore his great burden of professional tasks, domestic responsibilities, and physical ills so buoyantly that others almost forgot its magnitude and came at last to feel that he was fortunately of a nature to forget it himself in the occupations and attractions of each passing hour. It was difficult to conceive that, consciously shadowed by the very wings of Death, he could cherish ambitions so far-reaching, plans and projects so capacious, and such self-congratulations on the happiness of the present moment and the rich promise of the future.

Facts and feelings which would have paralyzed other men seemed to act as a stimulant on Richardson. Because to-morrow was uncertain he was bent upon using and enjoying to-day to the full. He felt that he must work twice as hard as though he were promised longer years; and he did thus work yet never seemed painfully pressed for time. With his uncertain health there could be little regularity in his hours of labor; but his power of laboring anywhere and at any time and under any conditions amply made up for this apparent drawback. He could work as well by night as by day, and as persistently on his sick-bed as in his offices or near his buildings — and often, he confessed, to better advantage there than amid outside influences and distractions. He took tremendous journeys at short intervals and at a rushing rate of speed, — sleeping night after night on the cars, spending day after day in the active superintendence of constructions under way or in dealing with those individual or corporate clients who are sometimes far less tractable than bricks and mortar, and at every odd moment, wherever he was, planning, inventing, designing, consulting, and deciding. Yet though he was always thus absorbed in his work, he was by no means wholly tied down to it. He had plenty of energy left to take an interest in other things, and that sort of energy which seems always to make time to gratify its wishes. His early taste for society never diminished, and the calls of friendly intercourse were met as only the half-idle are apt to meet them in this hurrying land of ours. There was no more frequent guest at the dinner-tables of Boston and its neighborhood than Richardson, none whose coming meant more surely a delightful evening, and none who was more certain to enjoy himself while delighting others. The hospitality of his own hearth and table was as unlimited as informal; and when his great offices had become one of the sights of Boston, no stranger ever failed of courteous entertainment there. The busiest home I ever saw, Richardson's was also the one where the doors were most generously opened and where the welcome seemed most heartfelt and perennial. And even in his rapid professional journeys he took care to arrange beforehand so that every spare hour might be devoted to those friends whom he would find along his path, and that many of the hours of actual labor might be made to yield their fruit in pleasant companionship as well.

Always ready to talk of himself and eager to talk of his work, he was neither egotistical nor narrow. His sympathies were very wide and sensitive, and his chosen associates were men who, while they understood his art and intelligently valued his achievements and his aims, trod themselves in other paths than his. Artists of one kind and another were, indeed, among them, but clergymen and literary men and men of business and of science stood just as near to him in friendship and served his intellectual needs as well. If the long list of their names could be given, it would show them all to be men of exceptionally strong and interesting individuality, but would also show that what bound them and Richardson together was the mere fact of this individuality — this personal worth or power — and not any narrower analogy between their peculiar gifts or aims or dispositions and his own.

It is another characteristic fact that even when he turned to books for refreshment it was not reposeful words he sought. There was little time in his life for desultory reading, but I remember his saying that when he was too tired and ill for work or social intercourse, — as just before his European trip in 1882, — he always wanted a book in his hand by day and under his pillow at night, and always the most exciting he could find; and I remember his naming Gaboriau's detective stories at the head of the list of those which had most satisfactorily met his needs.

CHAPTER V.

RICHARDSON's way of living showed an energy, a breadth of mind, and a fresh-ness of feeling which wrought their own well-springs of renewal. The fact that after and even during his working hours, he could turn to outside men and things with such eager interest, kept him young and sympathetic and alive in every fibre, and enabled him to do the work itself in a more fresh and vigorous way than would have been possible had he allowed himself to be exclusively absorbed by it.

Naturally, such receptive and assimilative power is a gift like any other. To all strenuous men life is made up of labor and of rest; but each must take his rest as nature has decreed he may, and only a fortunate few can take it as Richardson took his — in the way not of literal repose of mind and body, but of stimulating and fecundating action upon other lines. After a hard day's work in the office or a long journey by rail, and with half a night of labor still before him, to sit down at a big dinner-table full of diversely assorted guests and talk brilliantly and incessantly for a couple of hours on desultory themes, — this would hardly be refreshment for the average man. But "This is the way I rest," Richardson would often exclaim on such occasions, with boyish delight in his power to give truth to the words. Nothing about him was more remarkable than the manner in which he would then throw off his burden of thought and responsibility — unless, indeed, it were the manner in which he would take it up once more, fresh-ened by the interval but as wholly and deeply in his task again as though no alien idea had crossed his mind. Often, when one remembered his physical con-dition, it seemed as though it would need but a few days like those he persisted in living to exhaust him utterly. But again it seemed as though his will, his activity, his delight in life were what kept death at bay. Some one once exclaimed, "Richardson is all right — he will never take time to die"; and no words could more accurately express the feeling he inspired. It was only a few weeks before his death that after a round of his crowded offices he paused to say: "There is lots of work to do, isn't there? And *such* work! And then to think that I may die here in this office at any moment." But the words were so simply and bravely said, and he seemed to think so much more of the work than of the dan-ger, that the next phrase did not strike the ear as an unnatural sequence: "Well, there is no man in the whole world that enjoys life while it lasts as I do." Al-ways in the doctors' hands, he was certainly not what is called "a good patient," — the demands of the moment were too imperious with him for consequences to be often borne in mind. Yet if the wish to live, the imperious desire to get well, are indeed among the physician's mightiest helpers, Richardson aided his with a titanic hand.

The vacations he took were few, but he enjoyed them greatly and in characteristic fashion.

"In 1875," writes his intimate friend, Mr. Frederick Law Olmsted, "we went on a 'Cook's Tour,' together with our families, resting at Trenton Falls, Buffalo, Niagara, Montreal, Quebec, and among the White Mountains. It was the first vacation of his professional life, and was always afterwards referred to as his 'wedding journey.'

"The whole-heartedness with which he gave himself up to enjoyment for the time being was the most interesting circumstance of the journey. I have never seen the like of it, even in a school-boy. At Niagara this was shown in association with another quality. He refused to take part in discussing, or to consider at all how we should proceed, saying, 'This is a matter in which you are an expert, and I will not take off the least share of your responsibility.' And though my policy was the reverse of that which is generally adopted and which he would naturally have taken to, he showed no impatience, but made the most of whatever was enjoyable for the moment, never asking what was to come afterwards. We were out several hours without coming in sight of the Falls — did not see them fairly, indeed, till the next day. When we did he had caught the idea of throwing curiosity aside and avoiding amazement, and was willing to sit for hours in one place contemplatively enjoying the beauty, saying little of what was before us and chatting not a little of other matters, but taking quiet pleasure and laying up pleasure. At Quebec, on the other hand, he took command, and all the way to Montgomery he was studying the little old French farmhouses, and considering how much more pleasant they were than such cottages as we were accustomed to, in which so much more had been done to please."

In the summer of 1882 Richardson took the only long vacation of his later life. A European journey was decided upon, partly that he might be taken quite away from business and partly that certain specialists in London might be consulted about his health. His companions at the start and during many subsequent weeks were the Rev. Phillips Brooks of Boston, the Rev. William McVickar of Philadelphia, the Rev. Mr. Franks of Salem, and Mr. Jaques, a young friend from his own office. London, Paris, the south of France, and the north of Italy were visited, and then Richardson, accompanied only by his pupil, took a flying trip through the central and northern parts of Spain, going into some districts where even the architectural tourist seldom penetrates, but whither he was attracted, more strongly than to the Moorish provinces, by the presence of many Romanesque monuments little known to fame or the photographer. Mr. Jaques's account of the trip, recently written down from memory, runs in abbreviated form as follows : [1] —

"Mr. Richardson's enthusiasm carried him through as a traveler just as it did at home, and his wonderful vitality and endurance were never more fully tested than they were then. Mr. Brooks was a most tremendous traveler, and Mr. Richardson would not be outdone; and when I say that we visited thirty-three

---

[1] Mr. Jaques's long letter was kindly written for my information only; but his own words are so much more interesting than any paraphrase could be that I have ventured to use them with only such excisions as the necessities of space compelled.

towns in thirty-two days, it gives some idea of the rate at which we journeyed. Night or day it made no difference, and not until we reached Venice did it seem to tell upon him, though his great weight must have made it doubly hard for him. He was off for a holiday and was bound by no rules of health or diet, though they were all written down for him and I was supposed to enforce them! He rarely gave his impressions of things he saw except when in just the right mood, and would often be enthusiastic to a degree over some trivial point, and wholly silent over a magnificent work that impressed him tremendously.

"On arriving in London (July 1) he saw Sir James Paget and Sir William Gull, who took great interest in his case and pronounced his heart sound and his disease not necessarily fatal. They prescribed for him carefully and gave various directions, all of which he immediately began to disregard because he felt so much better over the results of their examination. He showed his desire to carry out their instructions more by hiring a landau by the week with a private coachman than by regularity of meals and hours.

"In London he spent much time in seeing the ordinary street sights, and visited very few historical monuments except Westminster and the Temple. The new Law Courts did not please or interest him, but he was greatly interested in the scheme of heating and ventilating in the Houses of Parliament.

"He visited Mr. R. Phené Spiers, whom he had known in Paris, and through him procured letters to Mr. Pullen, which gave admission to Mr. Burgess's house. Mr. Richardson went over it very carefully, but on the whole was rather disappointed in it, in spite of his great interest in Mr. Burgess. It did not come up to his ideal. At Merton Abbey Mr. William Morris happened to be in, and he went personally with us over the works and gave extremely interesting accounts of the progress he had made in the manufacture of his glass, carpets, stuffs, etc. He seemed to take great interest in Mr. Richardson and left his own party to drive to town with ours. The visit to Morris's house, and the five-o'clock-tea there on the following Sunday with the various 'æsthetes,' was an experience long to be remembered. De Morgan also showed him great attention, and Mr. Richardson had an unbounded enthusiasm for his work. He went through many of the new London houses, but was much impressed with their lack of interest and individuality. Burne-Jones was visited, and in fact all of the men whom we were told were 'unapproachable' received Mr. Richardson most cordially.

"The trip to Paris was made on July 13th. Then the running began. At midday on the 15th the start was made for Chartres, and the afternoon was spent there, Mr. Richardson being very loud in his admiration. At nine P. M. we were off for Le Mans, which we reached in the early morning. Monday morning at five we began a seventeen-hour journey to Clermont. Mr. Richardson was not especially interested at Le Mans, but Notre-Dame-du-Port, at Clermont, aroused all his enthusiasm, and he showed his persistency by routing out a photographer who was unwilling to be known, and spent the time up to the last moment in running over his coveted negatives.

"Of course the Auvergne churches were of particular interest to him, and he studied them critically, but silently for the most part — rarely talking of them save in the most general way.

"The journey from Clermont to Issoire was made at night, and after spending some time at the church (going to the hotel was quite out of the question), we took a four-in-hand for St. Nectaire. This trip has to be made to form any adequate idea of it. From the standpoint of pure pleasure in traveling it was the most delightful trip we took. Mr. Richardson was much interested in the little church in the clouds, and walked up the steep path twice to see it. He fairly raved over it as an example of early work — the more so, perhaps, as the others laughed at the rude structure and ungainly restorations. On returning to Issoire the church was again visited and an evening train taken for Brioude, where the cathedral was seen before breakfast and the nine o'clock train taken for Nîsmes.

"Next we went to Avignon and then to dirty old Arles with its vile hotels and lazy populace and lovely architecture. Mr. Richardson fairly raved over St. Trophime, and wanted to bring Norcross and Evans[1] over at once to see 'some really good work.' Some of the party would not stay over night, but Mr. Richardson insisted upon remaining so as to see St. Trophime again. He was charmed with its lovely carving and details.

"The trip to St. Gilles was very trying and disagreeable, but we were more than repaid. Mr. Richardson was not as much taken with the porch as at Arles, but spent much time in tracing the plan from the ruins. The travel now was very hard, and it was wonderful to see how his enthusiasm carried him along.

"At Marseilles we rested a day or two, and Mr. Richardson spent the time in shopping, as he was apt to do in the large towns. Thence we took the steamer to Leghorn and the train to Pisa. The Campo Santo occupied much time, and Mr. Richardson was much taken with it. As everywhere, all his spare moments were spent in getting photographs. The tower, cathedral, and baptistry pleased him immensely, and he studied them carefully from every point of view, and said that as a whole the group was the finest thing he had seen in Europe. One can imagine how its mere size delighted him.

"As one of the party was quite ill we settled down for a full week at Genoa. We explored all the out-of-the-way corners, finding bits here and there, bought lace, saw every junk-shop in town and hosts of paintings until we felt like natives. The next journey brought us to Florence, where we made a stay of several days. What with architecture, sculpture, and painting, and ice-cold lemonade on every street corner, Mr. Richardson's cup was full to the brim, and he would have stayed a year had he had his wish. He was much impressed with the staircase and court of the National Museum, and also of course with the frescoes in Santa Croce and elsewhere and the picture-galleries where he spent much time.

"From Florence an excursion was made to Siena and Orvieto. It was a great temptation for Mr. Richardson to go to Rome when we were so near, but he was deterred by the terrible heat. Bologna was then visited and a flying trip made to Ravenna, where we arrived just before noon only to leave again at dusk. Rest was out of the question. Not waiting even for food, we were off sight-seeing. Church and tomb, one after another, street after street, Mr. Richardson's enthusiasm knew no bounds, and even the long drive to Hadrian's tomb and St. Apollinaris did not suffice to exhaust him. From Ravenna back to Bologna, and then to

---

[1] The builder and the architectural sculptor to whom the execution of most of his work was intrusted.

Padua and Venice, did not occupy much time — sight-seeing by day and traveling by night.

"If Ravenna made Mr. Richardson silent and thoughtful, Venice had the opposite effect. He disregarded all advice, orders, and entreaties, 'went in for a good time,' — and had it. One dreaded to see the long 'schooners' of iced beer set before him, and order upon order for ices given at Bauer's. From early prowls almost at daylight until the midnight carnival on the Grand Canal, he was out and about and seemed to begrudge a moment's rest. The first thing after breakfast was always a visit to St. Mark's. Then a trip to Murano and the islands and a supper at the Lido, or long trips to odd corners in search of pictures, or hour after hour at the junk-shops, or whole mornings at Salviati's glass-works. Mr. Richardson wanted to buy the whole place, and could hardly be restrained from at least buying Salviati out. How he stood it all I cannot see. But though he did much more than any one of us he did not seem tired, while we were only too glad to crawl into some hole and sit down from sheer exhaustion. I was glad for his sake to get marching orders again and start for Padua and Verona. Yet even on reaching Verona at dusk he must go at once to see St. Zeno. Then, however, he gave in and was quite ill for a few days, but he soon recovered and was well enough to travel even on these ill days. Venice had filled him to the brim, and it was enchanting to see his genuine delight and almost childlike glee.

"In Milan he was confined to his room for two days, but passed the time in writing up his correspondence and preparing long letters to a building committee at home. He went wild here over St. Ambroise and tried in every way to get photographs of it. Here it was the party broke up.

"Crossing from Genoa to Marseilles, Mr. Richardson was very ill, for the boat was vile and the sea very high. He could take no breakfast, and, what with arriving late and spending a weary hour in the custom-house, we did not get to the hotel and food until four P. M. Yet he was soon ready to start again, and at eleven the next morning we were off for Perpignan, arriving there at midnight. The next morning we went on to Elne, and wandered through the lovely cloister, though we were not in very good condition to enjoy it. On reaching the lonely railway station, after driving through a wilderness of mud in a blinding rain, we found that the train for Barcelona did not stop there until the next day! But we made out that by going back to Perpignan at one we could leave there at five and reach Barcelona soon after midnight.

"Barcelona did not interest Mr. Richardson as much as some of the French towns, but he was very tired. A start at nine the next morning brought us at midnight to Saragossa. The next day, Sunday, we walked about the town and enjoyed thoroughly the lovely brick-work. Mr. Richardson was tremendously enthusiastic over the brick mosaics on the wall of La Zeo, and also with La Longa, which he called superb. It was here that we measured some brick-work and found the bricks one and one-eighth inches thick, while the joints were one and one-fourth. The tower of San Miguel and the one called *nueva o inclinada* also delighted him. And here too we found doorways with voussoirs eight feet long, — in the Pittsburgh jail one may see the effect. Taken altogether, Saragossa was so lovely that it whetted Mr. Richardson's appetite to press on. At Madrid the language got too much for us, and we engaged an interpreter who would take the palm in any country as a liar, but was so energetic that we saw a great deal with him that otherwise we should have missed. He was the man who told us, one cold night, that the train was late because the water had frozen in the locomotive boilers.

"In Madrid we spent most of our time in the galleries and in the lower quarters of the city watching the people. We made a trip to Toledo, and though the heat was excessive we 'did' the whole town and then went back to Madrid, sent our trunks to Burgos and started in light marching order — giving up the proposed southern trip and turning northward. To give an idea of Mr. Richardson's strength and endurance, here is another time-table : —

"We left Madrid at eight A. M. and arrived at Avila at three P. M. ; left there at nine P. M. and arrived at Medina del Campo at midnight.

"Then to a hotel until three A. M., and then (by the only possible train) to Salamanca at ten minutes past four, arriving at nine A. M.

"Avila was without exception the most quaint and interesting town we saw in Spain. The hotel had one large room with a brick floor and a great oak door through which the omnibus — that had evidently been in use two hundred years — drove directly into the house. Richardson was fairly overcome with delight in the cathedral; the spacing of the columns in the aisles in the apse was curious and most lovely, and it was here that he made the scheme for the plan of the Albany cathedral. He simply drank in every part of the building and was enthusiastic to a degree. The whole of Avila was charming, and great gates with eight or ten foot voussoirs abounded.

"Of course the cathedral at Salamanca (the old one) was of great interest to us, and we passed a great deal of time there. Mr. Richardson had never seen even a good photograph of it.[1] To Zamora we drove four-in-hand, but it did not take us long to make up our minds that in Spain, at least, the cars were preferable for night travel. There was much to interest us in this town, and in the cathedral we especially remarked the curious treatment of the tower over the crossing of nave and transepts. Next we took a roundabout journey to Toro, which gave us many weary hours of night travel. But the journeys in this part of the country were extremely interesting, and the very delays and vexations gave a certain novelty to the experience. At Toro we felt indeed in Spain. A clumsy chariot arrangement took us to an inn where the entrance was paved with cobble-stones and man and beast went in at the same door. On one side was the dining-room and kitchen and on the other the office and stores, while the whole rear was occupied by the stable — one long room with an earth floor and a manger running the whole length. Above this were the bedrooms. The cooking was all done with oil and plenty of it, and we were apt to leave our dinner almost untasted and stop on our drive and steal some grapes and buy sour bread to eat with them. The cathedral is extremely interesting and well placed, and all of these northern towns gave Mr. Richardson the greatest delight. At Toro the hotel-keeper, who had been there seventeen years, had never seen an American though several Englishmen had been

[1] It was the tower of the old cathedral of Salamanca that had given Richardson his idea for that of Trinity Church in Boston.

there. The rooms all had brick floors, and any article of linen was gone if it dropped upon them. But the beds were neat to a degree — always clean, and each sheet and pillow-case edged with lace. From Toro we went to Medina del Campo, where we walked about all day in a cold wind until midnight. Venta de Baños came next, and then Leon. Then Venta de Baños again, and then Burgos. All the trains were late and the travel very hard, but we had many amusing mishaps and experiences which relieved the monotony, though they tried our endurance and our tempers sorely. At Leon they were restoring the cathedral, and we were received very kindly at the architect's office, shown the working-drawings, and taken all over the building. If I remember rightly, the roof had fallen in and they were rebuilding the vaults. At an old church (I forget the name) the crypt was fine — great, fat, stumpy columns, strong, robust caps, and massive vaulting, just after Mr. Richardson's own heart.

"Though short and hurried in the extreme, our trip in Spain was most delightful. I may have given more idea of the hardships than of the architecture, but every day was full of pleasure and instruction, and Mr. Richardson drank in his fill of the lovely eleventh-to-thirteenth century work. Want of time and the hard travel were the only things that kept us from going to the extreme northwest where there were no railroads.

"We had a most charming ride through the Pyrenees to Bayonne, and left the next day for Poitiers. Here Mr. Richardson was fairly wild with delight. Notre-Dame and the houses alike filled him with admiration, and he raved over carvings and details for hours. From Poitiers we came to Paris, where we passed a week. Mr. Richardson looked up his old friends, especially Gerhardt, and had long talks with them. They were much interested in his work and not a little awed. He talked long and urgently about their giving up the old cut-and-dried-course and working out *their own architecture*. The arguments were entertaining, and Mr. Richardson threw his whole soul into them, but without avail. Public opinion was too strong and government positions too necessary. Of course we spent much time at the School, in the Louvre, Notre-Dame, and various churches, but did not make a business of sight-seeing.

"Then there was a social week in London, and the steamer for home was taken on September 27th."

It was a marvelous journey for a man in Richardson's state of health; yet it left him better in body, refreshed in spirit, and greatly strengthened in his art.

Such speed of foot as his must not be confounded with the similar rate at which the indifferent or merely curious tourist sometimes travels — though even he, I should imagine, not very frequently. When a man knows just where he wants to go and why, what he wants to see and exactly how, which things are essential and which superfluous, which are to be glanced at and which studied, and when his mind has been prepared for seeing and studying and remembering by previous professional training, a day in one spot will show him more, and leave permanently with him infinitely more, than a month could compass in the ordinary tourist's case. It must also be remembered that Richardson was not even an architect traveling to widen general knowledge by the sight of all possible architectural things so much as an architect who had a special concern with certain special things as bearing upon his already established manner of practice. When time permitted he took the most eager interest in work of every age and kind; but a single glance at a building could tell him whether or no he wanted — or, rather, needed — critically to examine it; and an hour's examination could teach him what he needed most to know about it. And the serious way in which he studied, despite perpetual haste, discomfort, and fatigue, is told in this passage from one of his letters home : —

ZARAGOZA, *August* 27.

" I know that I am getting great good from my trip, but at the moment, in the midst of it, I feel as if I were in a whirl, although I am doing things as thoroughly as I can by reading up before visiting places, and then reading while sightseeing, and studying again in the evening. To attempt to sketch would be folly as I have hardly time thoroughly to see things, which is a preliminary and indispensable forerunner to an intelligent sketch. I have seen too many sketches that were telling evidence that the sketcher had never properly seen what he thought he was drawing. I am constantly surprised at the lack of intelligence shown in choosing parts to be photographed; but probably I look at it as a specialist. . . ."

These letters — voluminous but very hastily written, often in pencil while actually *en route* — are chiefly filled with personal details and references to affairs at home, mingled with gay descriptions of the general aspect of the various towns, the peasants' costumes, the contents of bric-à-brac shops, and the laughable if tiring and annoying incidents of travel. They are therefore chiefly significant as showing how eager an interest he could take in every trifle that met his eye, exhausted though one might think he must have been by the double strain of incessant and uncomfortable travel and persistent professional sight-seeing. Definite description or estimate of the important things he saw does not frequently occur in them. Yet one or two citations will be of interest. While still in France he writes : —

" We started from Avignon for Arles at about eight o'clock in the morning. . . . St. Trophime was by far the most interesting portal we have seen and the cloister was charming, full of the nicest feeling. . . . In the afternoon of the same day we drove out to St. Gilles, a place noted only for the remains of its most superb abbey-church. It is glorious, and the ruins of the apse impressed me more than anything I have seen — and I don't forget its magnificent west entrance which for so many years has been my great admiration. To think that I have seen it and felt its influence so differently from the way one does from photographs ! Tell S—— that I feel as if I were being mentally and sentimentally stuffed with *pâté de foie gras*, and expect to have an artistic indigestion for the rest of my life unless he shakes things down a little for me when I get back."

And among the Spanish notes are these : —

" Zaragoza is a most interesting town — more so historically than artistically, though there are some fine things about the cathedral. The general feeling of the interior is noble and big, and it has a most charming octagonal dome beautifully studded in brick and tile, and a very interesting treatment of a wall-surface with slight panels made by projecting bricks and the back of the panels laid in cement-mortar and tiles (round green tiles), something like this.   [Sketch inserted in letter.]   The whole side of the northeast wall is covered with it and borders very delicately made with green, black, and yellow tiles all delightfully toned down by time. . . . Monday morning we left Zaragoza for Madrid at seven A. M. It was really cold.   The conductor of the train had on an Irish ulster — Spain in August !   On our way to Madrid we had some very striking scenery, desolate, bold, and grand ; and now and then we saw some of the most superb peaches and great black figs growing by the way.   A curious village — Saltillas — is built entirely under ground, and all we saw of it when the train stopped were the chimneys coming through the ground.   A most dirty, forlorn set of people as you ever imagined.   Yet I saw some pretty women. . . . [At Toledo] the cathedral is very noble and big, and some other very interesting churches but in very bad condition. A good bridge and guarded by the old Moorish gate — Puerto del Sol.   I saw there more Moorish work than anywhere else. . . . [At Avila] the cathedral is charming — beautifully studied, and quite captivated me.   There are many things here to detain one, but I had to go on, and saw San Vicente and the Dominican convent very hurriedly.   Our guide got us into the Dominican convent by lying to the monks and telling them we were Catholics — as I learned afterwards. . . . [At Salamanca] we went out, after having some bad coffee and goat's milk, to see the cathedrals, new and old.   Such a contrast between the two — the one small, old, simple, and beautiful, and the other — the contrary. . . . The drive round the fortified wall, with its round turrets now and then and picturesque houses, was very interesting, and I got a splendid view of the cathedral which composes very well with the new from the other side of the river Tormes."

CHAPTER VI.

LAST DAYS. — PERSONAL TRAITS.

During his early years in Europe Richardson had had neither the time nor the money to travel. He had then seen only northern work and comparatively little of that. As he was fond of saying, "he knew his Paris," but he really knew very little else except on paper. Now for the first time he was visiting the South with which his artistic nature sympathized far more deeply than with the North. For the first time he was seeing how men of like disposition with himself had worked in various lands and times; and in the western developments of Romanesque art he was studying forms and features which, as revealed in books and photographs, had already been embraced as his materials for self-expression.

Naturally he looked at them with an interest which a layman cannot fathom and which an architect with different leanings would by no means share — with a love and an intelligence immeasurably heightened by past experience and the prevision of future need. Many problems that had suggested themselves to him as new had, he now perceived, been long ago worked out by others. He often spoke of the singular delight it was to see "how those old fellows had done" the things he had been trying to do himself; and many qualities in their work impressed him far more forcibly than they had in pictures — qualities of simplicity and repose in general treatment as well as of exquisite refinement in detail.

This actual contact with southwestern Romanesque architecture established still more firmly his belief that it was the best source of inspiration for the modern artist. What had been a strong instinctive feeling, a passionately held and vigorously practiced faith, now became an assured dogma for which he could give much clearer reasons; and the special lessons he had learned showed at once in his work — not only in his plans for the Albany cathedral but also in the structures which he actually built. If we add to these gains the immense recuperation of energy and access of delight in labor which sprang from his long unresting rest, the renewed confidence in his powers and opportunities which grew from a comparison of his career with that of the average European architect, and the general broadening and freshening of his mind which were wrought by the varied scenes he had visited and the interesting persons he had met — if we add these other gains it will not seem strange that this journey should have been a second turning-point in Richardson's artistic life. With Trinity Church he had begun to do his true work; now, and only now, he was ready to do his very best work. Now, when there were but four years of life in store for him.

For some time after his return his health seemed better, and in consequence he thought less than ever about it and labored harder than before. Serious attacks of illness came now and then, but his recoveries were rapid and his strength seemed unimpaired. In the autumn of 1885, however, he was so ill that for the moment the gravest fears were felt, and when he was better again both journeys and social visits were forbidden. He was constrained to submit but most unwillingly, and his home was still constantly filled with guests and his hands were still constantly at work.

In March, 1886, he had a severe attack of tonsilitis followed by renewed danger from his chronic disease. His desire to go from home for change and rest was gratified, and though in New York he was so seriously ill that his physician was summoned from Boston, he rallied quickly and was allowed to go on to Washington " as an invalid," under strict orders against both friends and work. But an infringement of these orders brought on a second relapse, and he came home to sit once more at his own table and to look once more into his beloved office. When he went to his room it was never to leave it again.

The two weeks which passed before he died were weeks of infinite restlessness and pain; but he never complained and never lost his spirits, his hopefulness, or his keen interest in the work that was going on in the offices below. The day he died he talked confidently to his doctor about his tasks and aspirations, and declared once more that what he wanted was " to live two years to see the Pittsburgh Court-house and the Chicago store complete." These, he said, were the works he wished to be judged by, adding, with that frank self-appreciation the very frankness of which made it seem unegotistic: " If they honor me for the pigmy things I have already done, what will they say when they see Pittsburgh finished."

This last day (April 27, 1886) was full of suffering, but his actual death towards midnight was painless and peaceful. In its presence those who loved him most could only feel it was better thus than that he should have lived on, as with his disease he might, through many months of suffering, and of that enforced inaction which would have been still keener pain. Some of his absent friends had known the exceptional gravity of this last attack, but so strong was still their feeling that " Richardson would never take time to die," that even to them the announcement of the actual loosening of his imperious grasp on life came with as sudden a shock as though no warning had been given.

His funeral took place from Trinity Church, and the service was read by his close friend, Dr. Brooks. The respect and honor then expressed in private and in professional ways marked his passing as that of a man whose life had been of exceptional public value; and a similar feeling spoke from his fellow-countrymen at large through the pages of the general as well as the professional press. The death of no American artist had ever before been noted so widely, or with such clear recognition of its moment as a national misfortune. Richardson had so impressed himself upon so many minds in so many places that his loss — the loss of one who was a great architect and nothing else — was chronicled as that of a notable public character. Such a fact does not seem surprising if the matter is abstractly weighed. But as things had been in our country it was surprising enough to mark the dawn of a new day for art. It was an unexpected and thrice-welcome expression of that development of public interest in art which was the most important and happy result of his influential life.

In 1866 Richardson had become a Fellow of the American Institute of Architects, in 1879 of the American Academy of Arts and Sciences, and in 1881 of the Archæological Institute of America. Only two or three weeks before his death he received news of his election as Honorary and Corrresponding Member of the Royal Institute of British Architects.

If now a few more pages are given to his personal characteristics before the characteristics of his art are discussed, it is because an unusually intimate union existed between them. " The man and the work are absolutely one. The man is in the work and the work is in the man." [1] And, moreover, the outside work he did in addition to the actual creation of his buildings was quite as important as this and cannot in the least be understood unless one knows what manner of man he was.

No one could speak with him half an hour without perceiving that he had all the qualities which mark the born artist — ideality, fervid enthusiasm, keen perceptive powers, quickness of intuition, extreme susceptibility, and a passionate desire to express himself in creative action. Yet no one could know him at all well without seeing that there was a very marked practical side to his endowment too. Ideality he had in the broad sense of the word — imaginative power and inborn æsthetic feeling ; but he was no " idealist " as the term is used in current artistic parlance. There was nothing spiritual about him. His nature was robust, intensely human ; in the better meaning of the word, material. His intuition in art might carry him along so swiftly that for the moment he could give little distinct account of his reasons for moving as he did ; but they were as keen for the practical difficulties as for the abstract possibilities before him. Nowhere did his immense vitality show more clearly than in the strength of his imagination. Hopeful by nature, his imagination always seemed to give his hopes firm basis, and if disappointment came its effects were brief, for new and equally alluring prospects immediately opened to his eye. Yet even in his most imaginative moods he was neither vague, wild, nor utopian of idea. There was none of " the insanity of genius " about him. His fancy might take flights which to other minds seemed very bold, but it never led him into the cloud-land of the wholly unattainable. No one better knew the limits of the possible, only, being conscious of a greater power to work his will than most men can lay claim to, he set these limits farther off than most men dare ; and his imagination made the possible seem probable, or even for the moment actually certain. (It is of his schemes and ideas in art that I am speaking now ; — in his private affairs his imagination often ran away with his judgment, and he suffered the results in burdens and annoyances of many kinds.) No man ever loved art more sincerely, enjoyed it more passionately, or respected it more profoundly. But practical things appealed to him so strongly that one could not imagine him loving any other art half so well as the one he followed. I have already spoken of his keen feeling for the material serviceableness of an architect's work, and this feeling had almost as great a share in his respect and enthusiasm for that work as his passionate belief in its possibilities of beauty. To any eye he was the born artist ; but to the eye that

---

[1] Rev. Phillips Brooks, *Harvard Monthly*, October, 1886.

knew him he was the artist born to express himself in architectural language only.

This mingling of practical with imaginative and emotional qualities gave him a strong sense of humor — a sense which preserved him from those fantasies, affectations, and sentimental absurdities into which the purely æsthetic temperament often falls. A good story, a laughable incident, an expression where enthusiasm savored of bathos or which twisted truth to folly, was eagerly enjoyed even at his own expense — though never, it should be said, if at the expense of the dignity or the sacredness of art. Far from being embarrassed, he was greatly entertained by the notice his unusual size often attracted. He would tell with glee of certain days in Europe when the remarkable height of two of his companions and his own rotundity had excited an uncomfortable amount of popular attention — especially of one day when the street-boys asked " if the dwarfs were not coming too." He laughed like a Homeric hero when told of a German admirer of his works who as their architect was pointed out to him exclaimed, " Mein Gott, how he looks like his own buildings," declaring that after all " it was a great thing to be monumental." And he took a whimsical, or as he would vigorously protest, an artistic delight in having all his surroundings and belongings of corresponding size. Even his handwriting grew in size during his later years, and a letter from him with its large paper, huge black script, and enormous seal, was as characteristic as a glimpse of the man himself.

He bore his unusual bulk with so much ease and dignity that one never thought of speaking of it as one might in other cases. Richardson was " big " — that was all, and his bigness seemed appropriate to the general breadth and vigor of his temper, his manner, his ideas, and his creations. " He was large in everything — large in conception, large in soul, large in body. His presence filled the mind as it did the eye." [1] His face, moreover, had not changed so greatly as his figure, and had not lost the refinement which marked it in early life. It was a strong face and full of possibilities of passion, yet a very genial one and made singularly winning by the humor of his glance and the quick brilliancy of his smile.

Self-reliance resulting in great impatience under any species of control, and self-will pushed at times beyond the edge of self-assertion, were also very strongly-marked traits with Richardson. Naturally, to some men they sometimes gave offense ; but to all who were themselves manly and spirited as well as generous they seemed among his most attractive qualities. If he was wholly free from one fault that fault was affectation ; and it is only affectation which, when self-reliance and self-approval have any justification in fact, makes their expression censurable.[2] " Insist on yourself" is Emerson's teaching, as also that " a man is to carry himself in the presence of all opposition as if everything were titular and ephemeral but he." And it was a perpetual tonic to see one man whose inborn convictions gave

[1] Charles Francis Adams, Jr., in the Cambridge address already cited.

[2] " He was as entirely free from affectation as is Sever Hall. He was too large to be jealous of other men. ' I never saw it,' he persisted in saying about a big bad house of a brother architect which he passed every week in his life. He took people into the confidence of his ideas with his hearty and capacious ' don't you know ? ' He talked of himself and his work so largely that he was not egotistical." — Rev. Phillips Brooks, *Harvard Monthly*, October, 1886.

him this same teaching and who frankly and sturdily put it into practice; one man who knew his own value and was neither afraid nor ashamed to show he did, and who clearly conceived his own aims and believed in them so thoroughly that not to have tried his best to realize them would have seemed to him a treason to his art as well as to himself. Richardson's exuberant frankness and fearless self-trust refreshed one like a breath from some primeval clime. Perhaps there was about him a touch of " the barbaric " — it has often been said of his work at least. But if so, it was such a touch as we associate with the confident attitude and the naïf self-absorption of childhood, and had nothing to do with dullness of feeling. If he sometimes seemed too bold, too imperious, and not self-sacrificing enough, it was because he was more sure and eager, not because he was more hard than others; and in asserting himself as an artist, in claiming what he believed to be his rights and privileges and opportunities, he seemed so broad, so large, as well as frank, that he impressed one as making the claim for men of brains and men at work in general, and not solely and selfishly for himself. In his presence as in the presence of his works, one was often struck by the thought that, after all, the best manner to open a way for others is to make a wide path for one's own feet; that the best service a man can do his fellow-workers is to secure the noblest opportunities for himself, use them in the noblest way, and thus establish precedents which will be of perpetual profit.

Richardson was no philosopher and very little of a theorist in any direction. Yet he would often argue vigorously upon some such text as this, defending his independent, self-asserting course as that which all men — of brains, he meant — should follow. No man can do his best, he would say, unless he does believe in and assert himself; and what is he put into the world for if not to do his best? No man can do good work at all if he permits himself to be cramped and bound by the ideas and demands of others; if, in a favorite phrase, " he is perpetually thwarted." From this standpoint he would defend the former conditions of life in the South and the institution of slavery as well calculated to enable a man to express his nature fully, to " develop his own individuality." Of course he knew — though the knowledge did not interfere with his theoretic expositions — that no man, and certainly no architect, can fully put such a creed into practice, and that it would not be well for themselves or others if many should try. Yet he himself managed to live by it to a much greater extent than is often possible, and the spectacle was refreshing to all who could generously appreciate, first, the results he was able to accomplish, and, secondly, his own delight in their accomplishment. To those who really knew him for what he was it would have seemed a pity and misfortune indeed had Richardson been unsuccessful, and an impossibility that he should have been successful if so cramped, fettered, and " thwarted " as most of us must, and rightly should, content ourselves with being. One never quite judged him as one judges average men. A child of genius, it seemed but right that he should be the spoiled child of circumstance and friendship too.

Few men can ever have got as much from their friends in the shape of affection, of sympathy, of encouragement, and of practical aid. But he gave much in return, and even had he given less they would have felt rewarded in advance by the childlike confidence with which he looked for love and help. As a man regards a debt of honor more scrupulously than an ordinary business obligation, so Richardson's friends felt that his immense trust in their devotion could only be met with generosity. What he gave in return may be best explained in the words of one among them, also a distinguished artist, though in another branch than Richardson's : —

"I cannot express, or make those who did not know him even dimly understand, how much Richardson was in one's life, how much help and comfort he gave one in its work. It was not always that he could *do* much, but he would do what he could when other men would only have talked about it. And when he could not do anything he would yet take such an eager, unselfish, and really vital interest in one's aims and schemes, try so seriously to understand one's difficulties, and declare so imperiously that they must and should be overcome, be so intensely and intelligently sympathetic, give, in short, *so much of himself*, that he was the greatest comfort and the most potent stimulus that has ever come into my artistic life."

Even when one's acquaintance hardly justified the use of the word friendship the same effect was produced. He seemed at once so to grasp suggestions and ideas that they were clarified and illumined even for the speaker, and immediately to feel an interest which with others, if it came at all, would come by slow and gradual steps. And no matter how long an interval passed between one meeting and another, he was sure to be the same again, and one's intercourse could be taken up just where it had dropped, with none of that sense of change, loss, and waste which lapse of time and diversity of occupation so often bring. Even dwelling at a distance and seeing him but seldom, Richardson seemed a part of one's existence and not merely a casual feature now and again to reappear ; and when he died his furthest friends missed him as though he had lived next door. "The change which his death brought to his friends it is not possible to describe. It is a change in all their life. When some men die it is as if you had lost your pen-knife and were subject to perpetual inconvenience until you could get another. Other men's going is like the vanishing of a great mountain from the landscape and the outlook of life is changed forever. His life was like a great picture full of glowing color. The canvas on which it was painted was immense. It lighted all the room in which it hung. It warmed the chilliest air. It made and will long make life broader, work easier, and simple strength and courage dearer to many men."[1]

The impression made by his personality needed no help from any previous knowledge of his work ; — unidentified, he would just as surely have been noticed as a remarkable man. He was at once more interesting than any of his creations. There were greater things in him than any he did, and the fact showed at first sight and grew but the more apparent the better one knew him. And charm was as conspicuous as power in his bearing and address — was so conspicuous that the usual processes of feeling were often reversed with regard to him. Affection was the first sentiment to be born, and others followed if opportunity was gracious.

It is not easy to picture any congregation of men in which he would not have been the central figure. His great size marked him out no more than did his hearty, cordial manner, his fluent though slightly stammering speech, his eager

[1] Rev. Phillips Brooks, *Harvard Monthly*, October, 1886.

gestures, his jovial humor, and his brilliant smile ; and so great was the simplicity of his social attitude — so childlike his confidence that his presence was welcome and his words were valued, so outspoken his reciprocal interest and pleasure, and so pathetic his brave bearing of his physical disabilities — that no one thought of questioning his right to be honored and considered first. Affectation, — posing, — as already said, was wholly alien to his nature. No trace of the " social lion " ever crept into his manner and no tinge of lion-worship into that of his associates. Genuine, unaffected love and admiration were what he craved with peculiar longing and what he received in peculiarly lavish measure. The same word constantly comes to mind : great man though he was and polished man of the world as well, there was always something of the child about him ; and by this is implied, of course, that there was simple dignity as well as frankness in his attitude towards others. His enthusiasm of manner and abundance of speech never degenerated into familiarity or boisterousness. In any circle he would always have seemed one of the best-bred though one of the least stiffly conventional of men. Indeed, his manners were as noteworthy as any point about him. They were at the same time more cordial and more courtly than those of the average American, yet they seemed a part of himself and not a veneer. They were always the same and always right, no matter with whom he spoke. Some one once remarked that " if the Queen of Sheba were to come into Richardson's office he would give her but his usual hearty handshake, bright smile, and friendly word of welcome." But even a Queen of Sheba could not have wished for anything else — there was so dignified a manliness in his warmth of manner, so courteous a respect in his informality.

CHAPTER VII.

HEREDITARY INFLUENCES.

SUCH a character, temperament, and manner as the foregoing pages suggest we instinctively call " southern ; " and Richardson's personal appearance agreed so entirely with their evidence that one was apt to think of him as in no way akin to the men among whom his later years were passed. But, as we have seen, no New Englander of them all had in his veins more undiluted northern, more purely British blood. His own birth and his mother's, and the long residence of his father's family in an almost tropical island, justify his own constant claim that in fact and being he was a true son of the south. But the north begot him ; and it is from a union of just this kind that, alike in nations and individuals, the highest artistic powers have often sprung.

Nowhere do its good results show more clearly than in the history of architecture — that complex art which needs for its best exercise the blending of so many different gifts. I need only cite in illustration the architecture of the antique world, culminating on that soil of Greece where a new and more northern race dealt with the transmitted forms of Egypt and Assyria, and the architecture of the Middle Ages, reaching its most complete development in those districts around the capital of France where " northern energy and southern grace " met and agreed together.

Looking back at any period so far away as these, it almost seems as though the people as a whole had shaped the course of its constructive art and no individual artist had been very potent, while to-day it seems as though individuals were all in all and the nations nothing. In truth there must have been, alike in classic and in mediæval days, a more general artistic endowment than the modern world can boast, and a more complete unity in taste and feeling. Yet we may be sure that the disparity is not quite so great as at first sight it seems. It is only the lack of detailed records which conceals the constant presence in all earlier years of inspiring, directing, controlling personalities, while the conspicuous personalities of to-day will surely seem less isolated when time's perspective shall have set them further off. It can hardly be questioned, for example, that Richardson, despite his marked originality, despite the unexpectedness of his results and the intensely personal voice which seems to speak from them, did but express, more truthfully than we at first could think, certain ideas and tastes and feelings that were latent all about him. But however these things may be, it is in any case interesting to note that the union of northern and southern influences by which Richardson was moulded is just the union which we might expect to mould a great architect ; and it is encouraging to remember that by virtue of this union he was the more and not the less characteristically an American.

When, however, we are studying any man of marked ability, — and especially any man whose ability rises so high as to pass the line where talent ends and genius begins, — special as well as general questions of descent become of interest. We like to ask not only of his race but of his family, and we are pleased when, as is the case with Richardson, family records remain and speak with a voice which confirms belief in the " doctrine of heredity."

We have seen that his blood was on both sides of excellent quality ; for although his father's ancestors were never so conspicuously before the world as some of the Priestleys, they held an honorable place among the most respected citizens of Bermuda. Of his father we are told that " even as a school-boy his perseverance was such that he never failed to succeed in any branch he undertook ; " and that as a man he was distinguished by all the qualities which make one beloved by his friends and honored by his fellow-citizens. But we learn of no especial gifts which he or any Richardson transmitted to the architect except ability in mathematics. It is to the Priestleys, and above all to the famous doctor, that we must turn for signs of close intellectual and emotional likeness. No two men could have differed more widely in the use they made of their powers ; yet in natural endowment Richardson and his great-grandfather must have been near akin.

Priestley's activity was so very varied that it is almost impossible to class him. He was philosopher, theologian, politician, chemist, electrician, grammarian, and a dozen things besides. The most exact description one can give is that he passed his life in observing and in formulating, and that he brought these processes to bear now upon the soul of man and now upon the phenomena of the material world. Richardson was an architect and an architect only. His concentration was as marked as was Priestley's versatility. Yet he too had a richness of endowment that might easily have been turned to varied ends. His mind, as has been said, was very active, his intuitions were very quick and keen, his sympathies in a hundred things that lay well outside the field of architecture were easily aroused and for the moment very warm.[1] But the uncertainty of life was early brought home to him with peculiar force, his profession was of a peculiarly exacting kind, and all his practical energies were confined within its single channel. And very fortunately. His concentration meant that he did his best in the single branch he chose ; — not, perhaps, the absolute best that was in him, but the very best that each passing year of his short life permitted. On the other hand, long and strenuous as was Dr. Priestley's life, its results would have been of nobler quality had their quantity — or at all events their variety — been less. One need not credit or even consider all the special faults which contemporary adversaries noted in his work. It needs no examination to tell that, no matter how great his abilities, how intense his energy, a man who writes a hundred and forty-one books on almost half a hundred subjects needing serious study and prolonged experiment, cannot always have written carefully or wisely, and cannot have done his very best in any single branch.

[1] " He had quick sympathies with subjects of which he knew nothing. He gave one as much reason to believe as almost any one I ever knew that there is truth in the happy theory that all men have all faculties, and what faculties find their way out to activity in this bit of a life is largely an affair of chance, and that somewhere, some time, all faculties in all men will come forth into activity." — Rev. Phillips Brooks, in *Harvard Monthly*, October, 1886.

But apart from this difference in its direction, both men did their work in the same spirit. Indomitable energy was theirs by birthright — ceaseless industry, tireless perseverance, intense devotion to the task in hand. Both were workers for the sake of work: *Labor ipse voluptas* might have served as a motto for the one as truthfully as for the other. Each met with difficulties which might well have daunted him; but neither was daunted or turned from his path, or lost his childlike delight in life or in the success of his labors. And there is a singular analogy between Richardson's last days and those of Priestley when, as his son relates, he told his doctor, " that if he could but patch him up for six months longer he should be perfectly satisfied, as he should in that time be able to complete printing his works."

Priestley says in his autobiography that he had " an even chearfulness of temper " which " rarely deserted him even for an hour," and which he had inherited from his father, who " had uniformly better spirits " than any man he ever knew. This good gift he in his turn transmitted. Constitutional high spirits rather than an " even chearfulness of temper " is the phrase which best fits Richardson. But this only seems to make the likeness closer, for undoubtedly the stronger words would have better fitted Dr. Priestley too. When he paints his own portrait it looks mild and equable and cool enough, but his contemporaries give it much more pronounced and fervid traits. Again, we need not believe them wholly, and we may make some deductions from the words of the later writer who remarks upon that " indefatigable activity, that bigoted vanity, that precipitation, cheerfulness, and sincerity which made up the character of this restless philosopher." [1] No man who was bigotedly vain would have been so quick to retract his words when second thoughts had shown him a mistake. Yet he certainly never paused for second thoughts before rushing into print; his confidence in himself was unbounded and his impetuosity as great. Had his temper been very " even " he would have led a quieter intellectual life, and something more than mere " chearfulness " must have sustained him in the perpetual unquiet that he sought. There is every sign of a temperament quite like his great-grandson's, brought to even more pronounced development by the nature of his work. Words were his materials for self-expression, arguments his tools, while Richardson's language was of bricks and stones which give opportunity to declare and preach but no chance to argue, and which inculcate deliberate methods and the foreseeing of unalterable results. Yet even in Richardson's buildings it is easy to read the enthusiasm, the impulsiveness, the self-trust which he had inherited, and his speech and manner still more distinctly showed them.

Intellectual independence was also a trait which these kinsmen had in common. Neither ever accepted current beliefs because of their mere currency, or feared to express his own lest they be deemed " unorthodox." Southey calls the Doctor " a man who speaks all he thinks; " [2] another pen declares that " frankness and disinterestedness in the avowal of his opinions was his point of honor; " [3] and the phrases may here stand with a double application. It matters nothing that Priestley spoke with definite words and Richardson through the abstracter language of

---

[1] Lord Jeffrey, *Edinburgh Review*, October, 1806.
[2] *Life and Correspondence*, ch. v.
[3] Sir James Mackintosh, *Life*, i. ch. vii.

an art. Just the same spirit that guided the theological and scientific writings of the one inspired the artistic practice of the other. Everything was examined at first hand, tried in the balance of personal thought and feeling; and whatever was then believed was proclaimed without deference to any "doxy." Indeed, the bias with Richardson as with Priestley was towards the new and unfamiliar for the sake of its freshness, not towards the old and honored for the sake of its accepted title; and towards undue haste and over-emphasis in expression rather than towards a cautious reticence. Each of them, in short, was an originator, a leader in his own path; and this means that both were born to be independent, "heterodox," and combative, but means, too, that both were constructive and not destructive by nature.

Of course, with regard to Richardson, this fact is very clear, — the mere name "artist" is the proof. But if Priestley's story be fully read it is as clearly proved for him. Like his descendant he was an idealist, — a man with ideals in which he passionately believed, and to which he desired to give concrete existence. And if he was an iconoclast, it was because certain things stood in the way of those he wanted to establish, — not, in religion or in politics any more than in science, an iconoclast for the mere pleasure of destroying.

If it seems strange that two men so unlike in their vocations should have been so alike in nature, the explanation is that one of them was not by nature really fitted for the part he chose to play. Your true philosopher is not quick but slow and very patient, is not confident but cautious, is never emotional, rash, or hot, loves contemplation more than action, cares far more for knowing than for doing. It is the man of artistic nature who longs to be creative, who can hardly pause to know, so great is his desire to do, who passes lightly by the thoughts of others in his impulse towards self-expression. And it is he, too, whose mind is "objective" — loves concrete things, demonstrable facts, and definite decisions. The philosopher's mind is content with vagueness, shuns cut-and-dried definings, sees the highest virtue often in "suspended judgments," and disports itself by choice in cloud-land. Read now what a historian says of our philosopher : —

"Priestley's mind was objective to an extreme; he could fix his faith upon nothing which had not the indorsement of sense in some way impressed upon it. . . . The most spiritual ideas were obliged to be cast in a material mould before they could commend themselves to his judgment or conscience. His instinct was rapid to a degree. He saw the bearings of a question according to his own principles at a glance and embodied his thoughts in volumes while many other men would hardly have sketched out their plan. All this, though admirable in a man of action, was not the temperament to form the solid metaphysician, — nay, it was precisely opposed to that deep reflective habit, that sinking into one's own inmost consciousness, from which alone speculative philosophy can obtain light and advancement." [1]

But the artist is above all a man of action, of deeds; and no temperament could be more artistic than the one thus painted. More love of action than love of contemplation, and more perceptive power than reasoning power, — this seems

---

[1] Morell, *History of Modern Philosophy*, i. 142, 143.

to have been Priestley's character not only as a metaphysician but as a man of science too. And if it was the character of a Priestley who was by training and profession a philosopher, Richardson may with certainty be said to have been indebted for his talent to that maternal blood of which he always loved to boast.

In conclusion it is interesting to note that Priestley's portraits show a strong likeness to his great-grandson, not in general type or in coloring but in the shape of the forehead and the manner in which the hair grows above it, and in the peculiar line of the eyebrows — rising sharply towards the temples. Even the fact that Richardson's stammer was inherited from the Doctor (who regarded it as " a providential check " upon his " undue loquacity ") seems not insignificant as emphasizing their close kinship; nor the fact that the only one of Richardson's six children who has inherited the stammer from him has also inherited a face which still more nearly resembles the Doctor's than did his own.

CHAPTER VIII.

EARLY WORKS.

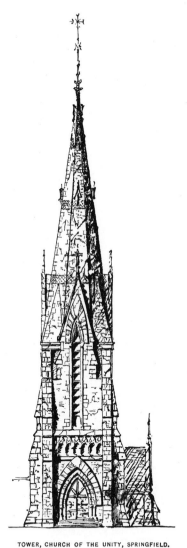

TOWER, CHURCH OF THE UNITY, SPRINGFIELD.
(Autograph Drawing by H. H. Richardson.)

THE manner in which Richardson began his professional life and gained his first commission has already been described. The Church of the Unity was a much more important piece of work than usually falls to a beginner's lot, and for Richardson the difficulties it presented were peculiarly great. He had been trained in Paris upon problems of a very different kind, and travel had not supplemented the teachings of the School. The ecclesiastical art of England was the study-book to which the taste of the moment in America distinctly pointed him. It is unlikely that he had familiarized himself with this art even upon paper, while he was of course without that knowledge of local materials, methods of construction, and business customs which most architects gain during a term of pupilage at home. The success of his effort is therefore doubly remarkable.

In general scheme the Church of the Unity is based upon a rural English type. It has no transepts or western portal, but has aisles and clerestory and at the southwestern angle a projecting porch above which rise tower and spire.[1] These are English in feeling, and the windows in all parts of the building are acutely pointed. But here analogies end. There is no effort after "scholarly" treatment according to any historic pattern. No mouldings or sculptured decorations are anywhere employed, the square-sectioned windows being merely surmounted by thin, flat drip-stones which have too much the effect of wooden features to be commended except for frank simplicity. And as the Unitarian service did not require it, there is no chancel.

It is most interesting to see how this first work reveals the essential qualities of Richardson's art, how it proves that what he thought most about was the building as a whole — the mass, the body — and not any one feature or any question of treatment or decoration. Other Gothic churches have been built in America which seem better than this if tested for evidence of academic knowledge or of a

[1] On account of the surrounding trees no good picture of the church as it appears to-day could be obtained.

sense of the beauty possible to individual features.   But we seldom find one which
is half so good in general conception and arrangement, which so immediately affects
us as a whole, an entity, or is so harmoniously massed, so graceful in silhouette.
Fortunately it stands apart from the neighboring houses on a slightly elevated
site and may be well seen from several points of view.   From each it is entirely

STUDY FOR CHURCH OF THE UNITY, SPRINGFIELD.

satisfactory as a composition, while all its lines bear clear witness to the disposition
of its interior.   The subordinate rooms which lie to the eastward are neither confused with the church proper nor dissevered from it.   Each mass has its own roof,
but the two roofs unite in a harmonious whole from whichever side they are
seen.   The porch beneath the tower is attractively designed, and the west front
is much more interesting than in the average English church where entrance is
effected through a porch.   A low aisle-like inclosed arcade runs all across it, forming a large vestibule which is of as great practical as artistic value.

Inside, both scheme and treatment are simple. There are no galleries, and at the west end there is nothing between the low doors that lead into the vestibule and the high-placed rose-window except a plain field of wall which, it is said, Richardson hoped might some day be covered by a great picture. The treatment of the east end is, however, individual and interesting. Choir-galleries and organ-pipes are placed in two groups above the pulpit, forming with it an agreeable composition and doing much to redeem that architectural nudity which the absence of a chancel involves ; and behind the pipes the wall is pierced in such a way that the organ may also be used for services held in the Sunday-school room beyond. The whole interior is colored on a very simple scheme superintended by Richardson himself. It is rather " hot " and shows no especially strong feeling for color, yet it has no trace of that crudeness or of that vulgar over-emphasis in tone which at this time still commonly characterized such work.

Outside, the red sandstone of which the church is entirely built is well treated, though not with the technical individuality that marks Richardson's maturer work ; and on the whole, it is a building the aspect of which would do credit to a later day and a much more experienced hand, while its practical success is heartily vouched for by its owners.

The next building Richardson designed — the railroad-offices close by the Boston and Albany Station in Springfield — is rectangular, stands on a corner site, and measures about one hundred and ten feet by sixty feet. It is four stories in height, with a mansard roof, and is built of light-gray granite — rock-faced ashlar with rusticated angles and cut trimmings. If we knew neither its date nor the name of its builder we should not think it especially interesting or individual, though it would reveal a much truer feeling for proportion and for repose and dignity than have often been combined in our commercial structures. Named and dated, however, it has points of great interest. It proves in the first place that even when thus fresh from his Paris training Richardson felt no wish to put the special lessons of that training into practice. Though in style it is " free classic," it is not " free classic " of any current Parisian type. It is a Roman Renaissance scheme of much the same sort as other American architects, very differently trained, have very frequently tried. Again, the boldness with which the rock-faced stone is used was much more remarkable twenty years ago than it would be to-day, and gives a hint of that feeling for " bigness " which, in technical as well as in other directions, so strongly characterizes Richardson's later work.

His next building was a charming little rural Episcopal church at West Medford, near Boston, the commission for which he gained in competition.

Here again an English type is in some parts reproduced, though again with no " scholarly " minuteness. The tower rises over the north transept and the main porch is towards the west end of the north side. There is a rose-window in the west end above a small plain door, and eastward a chancel (finished as a polygonal apse) the walls of which are of the same height as those of the nave but the roof much lower. The design has great breadth and simplicity, and the apse with its buttresses and high-placed arcade of small windows is an especially charming feature. The most noteworthy point about the building, however, is the nature of its material.   It was a bold but a sensible and artistic device to employ for its walls those loose, rounded stones which the retreat of the glacial ice left so thickly scattered over New England soil.

> "That is best which lieth nearest —
> Shape from that thy work of art,"

is advice which need not always be taken as the architect's rule of practice.   But it is certainly sound advice when economy should be consulted, and, intrinsically, the bowlders of New England were as well entitled to be put to architectural service as, for instance, those Norfolk flints with which old English builders produced such charming and such individual results.   Richardson was not the very first architect to use them, but the success of his church first conspicuously proved their artistic value.[1]   They are very vigorously and frankly managed, but very sensibly except in the spire where the outline is rather disagreeably broken by the over-prominence of certain units.   Cut stone is employed for the trimmings in sufficient quantity and with sufficient skill to give stability of effect and an appropriate degree of refinement.   Arches in which the outer line of the voussoirs takes a sharper curve than the inner line are not always agreeable features; but here their effect is good, for it increases the apparent strength of the arch, and with so heterogeneous a wall-fabric strength in the arch was particularly desirable.[2]

These are the three works which Richardson built before his association with Mr. Gambrill.

The first he built after that association had been formed, with the exception of a dwelling-house in Boston,[3] was the Agawam Bank in Springfield — a granite façade three stories in height with a mansard roof.   The doorway and the windows of the lower floor are round-arched; the upper windows are segmentally pointed; and in all of them the immensely heavy, rock-faced voussoirs differ still more conspicuously than at Medford in the lines of their outer and inner curves.   A very stumpy little marble column — its shaft not much deeper than its foliated capital — is everywhere introduced between the jamb and the arch. Naturally, such a building is conspicuous and striking; but it is striking as are countless others in all American towns where pure fantasy or a desire to do "something new" seems to have been the ruling motive.   And yet it gives certain signs of latent ability.   It is bad as a work of art but not bad in a weak, hesitating, or inconsistent way.   It is "all of a piece" and shows that though its designer was mistaken in his aim he knew very clearly what that aim was; and there is a rough, even brutal strength in the way its stones are used and treated which means an immature, exaggerated effort after valuable qualities which few architects at that day seemed to prize.

---

[1] The use of these bowlders was suggested to Richardson by Mrs. Brooks, one of the donors of the church. They had already been employed in building a barn on her country-place.

[2] The frank eclecticism of Richardson's work, even at this early period, is shown by his use of this kind of arch, which never occurs in English work of any historic period but is frequent in Italian.

[3] For the sake of clearness it has seemed best to leave all Richardson's dwelling-houses to be described in a separate chapter; and in the same chapter his railroad stations will also be noticed.

The High School building for Worcester, Massachusetts, commissioned in November, 1869, is also "nondescript" in style and quite different from any previous essay. It is a rectangular structure with a basement, two main stories, and a mansard with many dormers, with corner pavilions, independently roofed, and in the centre of the façade a bold arrangement of stairs and porch above which rises a tower finished with a very tall and slender spire. The main window in each face of the tower is round-arched, but all the other openings are square — sometimes single and sometimes grouped. All the horizontal divisions are strongly marked, and though the design shows minor faults it shows many points of excellence as well; and as a whole it has much more character — is much more of a conception — than either of the secular designs which had preceded it. A very noteworthy because at that time wholly novel feature was its decoration by pronounced surface-color. The main material was red brick, but black bricks, and red, green, and black tiles were profusely introduced, — as in the string-courses and between the dormers, — and vari-colored slates were used on the roof. A brother architect, writing to Richardson before the work was quite finished, says : —

"The High School I liked much. But the green tiles are not a success — too strong in color and not rich. Moreover they are not in harmony with anything else. The other thing that struck me as not right is the slating — its color. It is so arranged as to obscure the line of the cornice instead of making it more distinct. It takes some study to distinguish the red slates from the red brick of the dormers, and both together make a red surface which looks like wall. I think the slates between the dormers should have been black or green. The towers and roof and all that, seem to me a success, and I think the Worcester people will like it when they are used to it. But they will not get used to the green tiles. At least I should not. The use of black bricks for surface decoration is interesting, and I am glad to see it done. But I should hesitate about copying it. It looks a little poor as well as flat. The tower promises to be stunning and the corner pavilions are much improved from the sketch."

An exhibition-building for the town of Cordova, Argentine Republic, was commissioned in November, 1869. It was a wooden structure, not very large, which was carefully put together in a vacant lot in New York, taken to pieces again, and shipped to South America with a number of carpenters who superintended its final erection.

The commission to build the Brattle Square Church [1] in Boston for a Congregational Society was gained in competition in July, 1870.

It is a cruciform building, not very large, with a lofty tower which stands in the angle between nave and transept, resting upon four piers connected by great round arches. The carriage-porch which is thus formed opens into a low arcaded portico or vestibule that is built out, flush with the face of the tower, from the end of the transept. This arcade and all the large windows are round-arched, but a range of grouped square-headed lights occurs, beneath a large rose, in the end of

[1] This name is a mere survival of that by which the congregation's earlier place of worship had been known. The church stands on the corner of Commonwealth Avenue and Clarendon Street.

TOWER, NEW BRATTLE SQUARE CHURCH, BOSTON.

the nave. The roof and louvre-boards are covered with red tiles, the frieze and the capitals in the porch are of a light-colored stone, and the angels' trumpets are gilded. A single kind of stone appears in the rest of the structure — in walls and trimmings alike — and the treatment of its surface does not vary. But it is a pudding-stone of a warm yellow tint conspicuously diversified with darker iron-stains, and such good advantage has been taken of its changing tone to avoid monotony in the fields of wall and to accent the trimmings that the general color effect is both rich and animated.

Nevertheless the church is not, as a whole, a successful piece of work. No part of it is very interesting except the tower, and though this is in itself superb it has little organic relation to the lower masses and crushes them by its excessive size and stateliness. Its chief intrinsic beauty is its chief defect as a feature in such a composition. I mean its magnificent independence — the way it rises in a single spring from its own sturdy feet. Disdaining the support of the adjacent walls it deprives them of dignity, and would itself appear to better advantage if they did not exist, — if it stood in actual as it does in virtual independence. And there was once a chance that it might thus stand. The church was a partial failure, not only from an artistic but from a practical point of view. Its acoustic properties were bad, and when — for reasons of poverty and of decline in numbers incident to their removal to so distant a site — its owners were compelled to abandon it shortly after its consecration, it remained unused for several years. In 1881 it was bought by a private purchaser, again offered for sale, and saved from destruction by the generous action of a few citizens, who subscribed a certain sum towards its purchase on condition that the tower at least should forever be preserved. Richardson always said that the acoustic difficulty might be overcome by the building of galleries, but was not allowed by his clients to try the experiment. It has been tried, however, and with the best success, by its present owners (the First Baptist Society); and there now seems little prospect that the proposal so often made while the church stood idle will be carried out — the proposal that its body should be pulled down and the site planted as a little park, leaving the tower in isolation like one of those Italian campaniles to which in outline it bears so strong a likeness. It is quite certain that Richardson himself would not have been displeased to see this done. Nothing about the church satisfied him except the tower, but for this he had an especial liking, and its voluntary redemption by the people of Boston pleased and touched him deeply.

There is scarcely another work of his which could be criticised as this church must be. His most constant merit as a designer was his power in general conception — the way in which he first " got his building " as a whole and then got its features, working so that each feature should have its due relative importance and no more, and that all should act together to the enhancement of the main architectural impression. And even here, if we consider the tower in and for itself, we find this characteristic merit proved. Judged in itself the tower is good and impressive as a whole — not by virtue of the separate excellence of certain features. Perhaps to some eyes its chief charm may seem to lie in its great sculptured frieze. But it does not; it lies in the main conception and in the artistic concord of all other features with the frieze itself. It is their appropriateness to the place they hold, their right effect as portions of a large design, which makes the sculptures so imposing. The tower does not exist for them but they for the tower, and their own beauty is accented by the fact. The frieze was modeled by the French sculptor Bartholdi in Paris, but the general idea for it was Richardson's, and the carving was done by Italian workmen after the stones were in place.

A mixture of diverse elements — French and Italian, ecclesiastic and secular — shows in the various features of this church. But Romanesque forms are paramount, and, though they are not treated in at all the same spirit which Richardson's later works reveal, they give the building extreme importance as the first which in any way predicts the ultimate course of his development.

A large State Asylum for the Insane, to be built at Buffalo, N. Y., at a cost of two million dollars, was commissioned (in competition) in March, 1871. It has a central pavilion, with two towers of moderate height and a recessed porch of three round arches, flanked by long retreating wings. It is dignified and creditable as a composition, but its chief excellence lies in its plan, which Richardson adapted from a French prototype.

CHAPTER IX.

EARLY WORKS.

STUDY FOR NORTH CHURCH, SPRINGFIELD.

RICHARDSON's next work was the Hampden County Court-house at Springfield, Mass., commissioned (in competition) in July, 1871. Here again Romanesque features are conspicuous, although they do not preponderate in the general effect. And here again — and more appropriate because put to secular service — is the machicolated cornice which speaks of a study of the fortified palaces of Tuscan towns. Appropriately, too, it is accompanied by forked battlements; and if Richardson had been permitted to carry out his original intention, the body of the building would have been protected by overhanging eaves, supported by great brackets in the mediæval Italian way. The present set-back cornice was the result, and not an entirely happy one, of his determination to have a very emphatic feature of some kind, even if not of the kind he preferred.

The building stands free on all sides, though not far enough from its neighbors to be very advantageously seen, and is built throughout of granite. Its depth is much greater than its breadth on the two main streets; therefore the ends toward these streets are designed as great pavilions, and the central connecting portion is somewhat deeply recessed between them. The entrance façade forms, of course, one of the shorter fronts. The roof with its dormers and the tower group well together, and the tower grows organically from the lower mass. It cannot be said that all minor features are so fused together and so infused with individual feeling that they form an architectural conception in the truest, best sense of the word: and some of them are palpably discordant — like the steps, which are not very dignified in themselves and not well united with the loggia; and like the balcony, which sadly weakens the most conspicuous corner. Yet it may be said that in general they harmonize fairly well, that they work together to give one the impression of a dignified building and not of an aggregate of disconnected parts. The chief Romanesque motive — the loggia — is treated feebly, if we take Richardson's own later manner as a standard. But the mere introduction of such a motive was a piece of bold originality at that day, and the whole design was then so novel and so much stronger than the average of such designs, that we cannot wonder the Court-house made a deep impression and was thought to promise a great future for its author. Even to-day it would be counted a more than creditable work for so young a man.

To my mind the best part of it, and the part which is most truthfully prophetic, is not the more elaborate façade, but the rear — which is very plain, frankly utilitarian in accent, yet so massive, dignified, and well-proportioned as to be really monumental. It shows how much may be done for the simplest walls by carefully designed, strongly battered foundation-courses. No device was used by Richardson more constantly or artistically than this, and there is none which plays a greater part in explaining the admirable sturdiness of all his structures.

The dated list which has been prepared for this volume from the old office-books of Richardson's firm gives the year 1868 as that in which the North Church at Springfield was commissioned. But the design then prepared was for a new building on the old site, and it was afterwards decided to build upon a new site. The present church was not begun until June, 1872, and its character proves the preparation of a fresh design, for it is much more akin to Richardson's later works than either the Brattle Square Church or the Court-house. It is, in fact, the first of his buildings which can be called really characteristic. Here for the first time speaks the Romanesque spirit as he afterwards so consistently expressed it — somewhat crudely voiced and not unmixed with other accents, yet unmistakably the same.

It is not in grouping and outline that one finds the church thus characteristic. But the composition is very good of its kind, the tower being well adapted in size to the lower masses and well connected with them, and having, with its spire, a strong and graceful silhouette. All the features of the tower are concordant, the transition from square to octagon is especially well and simply managed, and this portion of the design, at least, seems distinctly Richardsonian in idea and treatment. It is especially interesting to note the unconventional yet fortunate way in which the tower windows are treated. The turret impinges too much on the lateral face of the tower for the window to hold there the same central station as in front. But instead of making his window smaller, Richardson preserved unity and simplicity by making it the same in size and shape and pushing it boldly aside, almost to the quoins. The effect is piquant but has no touch of willfulness, for it at once explains itself as sensible.

The entire building, spire and all, is of red Longmeadow sandstone and the roofs are tiled. The nave, which is without aisles, measures one hundred feet by sixty feet and the transept eighty-four feet by forty-four feet. The contract price was forty-eight thousand dollars and the actual cost but little over fifty thousand dollars. Severe simplicity of treatment was therefore prescribed. But this simplicity is so frankly confessed for what it is, and secures so much grace as well as strength of effect, that it not only satisfies but charms the eye. The witness of the North Church alone should be enough in the eyes of any observer to put the claims of cheap elaboration forever out of court.

The Phœnix Insurance Company's building in Hartford, Conn., commissioned in March, 1872, does not call for detailed description, though it was interesting and influential in its day as another attempt at pronounced color-treatment. It is built of yellow, red, and black bricks with freestone trimmings.

The American Merchants' Union Express Company's building in Chicago should be included here among Richardson's early works, for, although it was commissioned a few months later than Trinity Church, it was built before the construction of this had had its influence upon him. It is dignified and in many features very good, and it shows a use of Romanesque motives which entitles it to rank as the first of his commercial structures that can be called characteristic; yet it is still "nondescript" rather than consistent in style.

With the exception of two or three dwelling-houses these buildings are all that Richardson designed in his first or tentative period. He began no others until Trinity Church had been given three years of his life.

A survey of this tentative period may offer some surprises to those who have known Richardson's art mainly in its maturer phases. So great in later years was his consistency in aim, feeling, and manner, that it is natural perhaps to expect to find something of the same consistency marking his very earliest efforts. But we do not find it. His early buildings, taken as a whole, do not foreshadow those whose list begins with Trinity Church, and though characteristic features now and again appear, it is not in such a way that at the time any certain prophecy could have been gathered from them. First one scheme is tried and then another. Often it is a scheme which may best be described as "nondescript," and whatever its nature it is never so repeated or reëchoed as to show a desire to work out its possibilities with thoroughness. A more diverse, more palpably experimental series of buildings it would be hard to find from any hand. In short, we see that in these earlier years Richardson was simply feeling his way — and towards what, he could not himself have told. He was also feeling it more cautiously than in retrospect may seem quite natural. If we except the tower of the Brattle Square Church, he made no experiments of so "big and bold" a sort that, even if unsuccessful, they would seem quite in keeping with his later big and bold successes.

Yet none of his work is really weak or timid, and it all looked a good deal bigger and bolder when it was built than it does to-day. This is a point which we should never forget: the great advance, both in vigor and in skill, which we have made in the last twenty years largely through Richardson's own influence. When we admire, although with reservations, this early conception or that, when we approve the vigorous treatment of his surfaces, when we delight in the beautiful color as well as form of the Brattle Square tower, when we appreciate the daring but wise because appropriate use of cobble-stones at Medford, even when we smile a little at the almost brutal over-emphasis of the chisel's work in the Agawam Bank, or at the crudeness of the color-scheme in the Worcester High School, we must remember the epoch when they were built and what were then the average efforts of American architecture. Only thus can we recognize how forcible and individual were in reality most of Richardson's early efforts.

Moreover, if we keep in mind the special circumstances of his own life and education, their testimony to his artistic nature as we knew it in after days grows much more clear. Judged as the products of a young man fresh from years of study and work in Paris, they show him daring and original enough. Most of his contemporaries, if they had been trained at all, had not been trained in any one kind of design, and with no recognized leaders before them were almost driven to pursue a widely tentative course. But Richardson had been thoroughly trained in an artistic creed held with absolute faith by a whole nation recognized as the most artistic nation of the modern world. The mere fact that this creed had taken no hold whatever upon his artistic conscience certainly proved that he had neither a conventional nor a pliable mind, while the fact that he did not at least cling to it for safety proved that he had a bold and self-reliant nature — safety might so well have seemed the highest attainable good amid that unfamiliar American confusion which meant little more than a confusion of sins and failures. The strength of his desire for self-expression and also of his belief in his creative power could not have been more clearly shown than by his instant and entire abandonment of Parisian formulas, illustrated by a remark he often made in his earliest New York days : " It would not cost me a bit of trouble to build French buildings that should reach from here to Philadelphia, but that is not what I want to do." Knowing his disposition, one feels sure that a theoretically developed belief that French buildings were not suited to American wants did not play much part in calling forth such words. He was never a theorist about himself except in retrospect. Not until he had practically found what he thought would satisfy American needs did he try mentally to define these needs. Not until he had begun to do his true work did he put into definite thought his idea of what an architect's work here and to-day should be. Instinct was his guide, experiment his test, and the first goal he sought was something that should thoroughly please himself.

The tendencies thus shown in his earliest works are the same which showed in his latest ; and they were tendencies which even while they resulted in but partially successful works proved him at once a born artist. It does not impugn but establish the vitality of his talent to say that he himself did not know at first whither it would lead him, and that it developed through experimental action, not by feeding upon theories. And it illustrates the purely artistic character of his mind to say that he was not only able but eager to submit himself to the leadings of that talent in spite of a training which had inculcated a very different course of action — to submit himself to its leadings and to try through a series of partial failures for something that would express it better than those Parisian patterns with which he might easily have secured a stereotyped success.

Nor, after all, did he need to experiment many times or long. His tentative period was wonderfully short considering how much it taught him, and the marked diversity of its products each from each proves a singular keenness of perception with regard to his real wants. He experimented during five years only, and he never once thought he was on the right path until he really got there.

Of course this was owing to the fundamental benefit of that Paris training the superficial influence of which he had so instantly shaken off. His schooling had not taught him what was right (for him), but it had made him able quickly to recognize what was wrong. An untrained mind would never have seen its own missteps so instantly, or so soon have found and rapidly assimilated the wholly unfamiliar elements out of which it could create success. Nor, it is almost needless to add, would an untrained mind have been able to secure fundamental qualities of excellence even in results which did not satisfy its aspirations. Richardson threw aside as useless the schemes upon which he had worked so long in Paris, but it was their careful study which had developed his feeling for proportion, his power of composition, and his appreciation of technical beauty to such a point that, dealing with wholly unfamiliar schemes, he could make his very first work admirable in mass and outline, could skillfully manage the great Brattle Square tower with its difficult decorative feature, could charmingly reproduce in small upon his Court-house the huge towers of mediæval Italy, could feel the full importance of such minor constructive features as the profiles of foundation-courses, and could at least try to treat all surfaces in an interesting and appropriate way.

In truth, the more we consider the conditions amid which he began and the preparation he had had, the more vigor and individuality and power Richardson's early works seem to reveal. And if they do not reveal quite so much of either quality as we might expect, or show so much clearness in aim and consistency in effort, is it not rather because our instinctive demands are exaggerated than because his development was inconsequent? The results of his life as a whole show that he was a man of phenomenal power. But would he not have been a man of miraculous power had he come twenty years ago fresh from the schools of Paris with a ready-made anti-Parisian creed and at once begun to build successful " original " structures, very various in purpose but consistent in themselves and among themselves to the precepts of that creed?

CHAPTER X.

TRINITY CHURCH.

THE site selected for Trinity Church was one which cramped the architect in his search for a scheme, but which promised him unusual advantages of effect if he could find a fitting scheme. It lay on one side of a large, irregularly outlined square, where the Art Museum had recently been built and where other structures might be expected which in size at least would be monumental; and it was entirely isolated — projecting into, not flanking the square, and thus having a street of average width on only one of its sides. But it was in the shape of a triangle of which the base-line formed by this street was almost as long as the other two.

This fact, however, which to an architect preferring the familiar Gothic type of church would have seemed unfortunate, was extremely fortunate for Richardson. It almost prescribed a design based upon the examples of that southern Romanesque which he had just begun to study. A church with a long nave and a dominant entrance-front could hardly have been well fitted to such a site. A compact ground-plan, a pyramidal mass, a tower equally conspicuous from all points of view — these were plainly the things to be desired. These Richardson secured, and so very skillfully that his church now looks as though its situation had been chosen expressly that it might show to the best advantage.

It is cruciform on plan, but all of its limbs are of nearly equal breadth — roughly speaking, fifty feet within the walls — and while it measures one hundred and twenty-one feet from end to end of the transept walls (outside), it measures only one hundred and sixty feet from the apse wall to the façade. The main ceilings are sixty-three feet and three inches in height, and the flat ceiling of the tower is one hundred and three feet and two inches. The tower is supported by four great piers, set near the angles of the crossing, which measure something over thirty-six feet to the springing of the arches that connect them by a clear span of forty-six feet and six inches. Narrow aisles, used only as passage-ways, add nine feet and four inches to the width of the nave, and its clerestory is borne by an arcade of two arches. Within this arcade, above the aisles, is a narrow triforium-like passage connecting the galleries which are built across the ends of the three limbs. The chancel proper is very short, but the apse is very large (giving the east limb a length of fifty-seven feet), semi-circular, and pierced by a range of tall windows set well up under the cornice.

An interior designed in some such way as this is certainly better suited to modern needs than one in which rows of columns intercept the sight and space is gained by longitudinal extension. Other American architects had already recognized this fact and had tried to give it acceptable expression. But Trinity was the first important American church which proved that it might be expressed with great architectural beauty and with an effect as truly ecclesiastic as that of the "long-drawn aisle;" and the influence of Richardson's success upon subsequent practice has been very powerful. It is impossible to say how strong with him was consciously the weight of practical considerations at the outset. The mere æsthetic factors in his problem were sufficient, as has been shown, to have alone determined his conception. But one cannot doubt that he at once perceived and welcomed the fact that the claims of convenience and of exterior

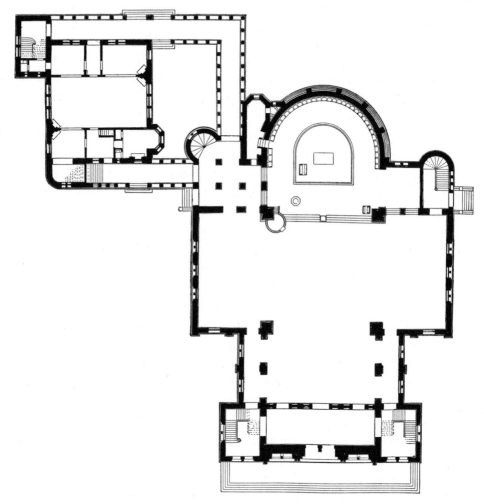

PLAN OF TRINITY CHURCH, CLOISTERS, AND CHAPEL-BUILDING.

beauty pointed in the same direction; and he certainly nowhere sacrificed practical to æsthetic interests, and only in a single feature sinned against entire appropriateness of expression. The church would be far less beautiful, inside and out, and no more convenient were the chancel smaller. But, expressionally speaking, it is too large a chancel for a very "low-church" service. In his usual optimistic way Richardson thought that when the chancel was once built its owners would be tempted into furnishing and using it in an appropriate manner. But this hope was unfulfilled, and to-day the chancel has a look of uselessness which is certainly to be deplored. Yet its intrinsic beauty — its purely artistic rightness — is so apparent that the sternest critic can hardly regret that in its design Richardson somewhat transgressed the great architectural law of "fitness."

TRINITY CHURCH, BOSTON.

As regards the construction of the interior, it will be best to quote from a professional pen : —

" The ceilings of the auditorium are of light furring and plaster in the form of a large barrel-vault of trefoil section, abutting against the great arches of the crossing, which are furred down to a similar shape, with wooden tie-beams casing iron rods carried across on a level with the cusps of the arches. The four great granite piers which sustain the weight of the tower are encased with furring and plastering, finished in the shape of grouped shafts with grouped capitals and bases. The whole apparent construction is thus, contrary to the conviction of the modern architectural moralist, a mask of the construction. We do not propose here to enter upon the question as to whether or to what extent the architect was justified in thus frankly denying his responsibility to the ethics of design as practiced and expounded by the greatest masters, ancient and modern ; it suffices . . . to note that the material of actual construction being nowhere visible in the interior to afford a key of color to the decorator or to affect his designs in any way, he had before him a field peculiarly unembarrassed by conditions."[1]

And it should be added that Richardson had such a state of things in view from the beginning. What he contemplated from the outset was, as he said, " a color church," — though it is not so easy to decide whether he was led to the idea by actual preference or adopted it as the best expedient which the money and the decorative processes at his command permitted. But, however incited, his masking of the construction was frank, consistent, and entire. Except for the division of the ceiling into narrow cross-sections by moulded strips of dark wood, it left the decorator a field as fortunate as free ; and this field Mr. La Farge, though working under great difficulties as to time and cost, utilized in a way which entirely justified the wisdom of Richardson's idea.[2]

The acoustic properties of the church proved good. It was a nervous moment for Richardson when the scaffoldings were removed and the preacher's voice was tried. His partial failure with the Brattle Square Church was still fresh in men's minds, and he knew that no degree of purely artistic success would be thought to redeem a second want of success in this great practical point.

The church is placed so that its entrance front faces the point of the triangular lot and overlooks the broadest part of the square, and is set back to the street-

[1] Henry Van Brunt: " The New Dispensation in Monumental Art," *Atlantic Monthly*, May, 1879.

[2] " Although it was often suggested during the progress of the work that the great piers at least should show the stone face apparent in the church, this has, nevertheless, from the first conception of the design, seemed in many ways undesirable, and propositions looking to that end have been, after careful consideration, always finally rejected. A rich effect of color in the interior was an essential element of the design, and this could not be obtained in any practicable material without painting. Brick-work, which might have been strong enough in color, would not have endured the strain upon it, and the use of granite was a necessity of construction. The cold, harsh effect of this stone in the midst of the color decoration could not be tolerated, and as between painting directly on the stone and plastering it to secure a smooth surface, it seemed decidedly preferable that there should be no difference in texture between the piers and the other walls, but that all should be plastered alike. The commonplace criticism, that plaster ' conceals construction,' can hardly be considered to apply here, for the piers and arches being simply portions of the wall, it would be difficult to show any reason for plastering the other walls which would not apply equally to the piers ; and that the inner surface of the walls must in all cases be exposed is a *dictum* from which the most conscientious would shrink." — Richardson's *Description of the Church* in the memorial volume published at the time of its consecration.

line which forms the base of the triangle. Its dependencies — chapel and Sunday-school rooms — stand towards one corner of the site, sufficiently removed from the main mass to mark their character and to leave its own outlines undisturbed from most points of view, but skillfully united with its eastern end by a small cloister-like space surrounded by a covered walk which is continued up the chapel-building as an external stair.

A vestibule stretches across the entrance front and is prolonged to a breadth of some ninety-three feet, forming the lower story of the western towers, which thus rise free of the nave. But as it stands this west end is still incomplete. The cappings of the towers were once built, but proving unsatisfactory were taken down, and the proposed deep porch has never been begun. If towers and porch were complete as Richardson designed them before his death the faults in Trinity's exterior would largely be redeemed. In a lateral view the nave lacks sufficient dignity, and in a western view the great tower and the façade come so close together as somewhat to confuse the eye.[1] From every other point of view, however, the tower (which without the finial rises one hundred and fifty feet) groups beautifully with the lower masses — strongly asserts itself as the most important feature of the design, yet in such a way as to dignify and not crush the rest.

The yellowish-gray granite employed throughout for the rock-faced ashlar is soft and warm in tone, having much the effect of a sandstone. The trimmings are of that red Longmeadow sandstone which by its admirable texture and beautiful color has done so much for Boston buildings. The lower roofs are of plain slates, the roof and louvre-boards of the tower of semi-glazed red tiles, and the crockets of red terra-cotta. The pronounced yet harmonious effect of color thus produced is one of Trinity's greatest merits and at the time when it was built seemed the most boldly novel of them all.

But the Trinity we see to-day is a very different church from the one the building-committee chose. During the progress of his work Richardson so recast it that little of his first conception remains except the chief features of the plan, the general proportions of the limbs of the cross, and the general treatment of the chancel — which last was not changed save by a simplification of its windows.

In these windows the competition-drawings show a more complex section for the arches, and lateral shafts in each light. In the transept-ends they show a single great window — somewhat of the same type that had been used in the

---

[1] " Some changes in the design were made as the work went on, in compliance with real or fancied necessities of convenience for construction, and . . . the modifications of outline required by the change in proportion of walls and tower thus made can hardly yet be considered as fully carried out, so that the actual building at present lacks, perhaps, the unity of the original design without attaining a new unity of its own. Especially is this the case with regard to the western towers ; a lowering of the church walls, made in hope of affording an additional guarantee of good acoustic quality in the building, which was felt to be a paramount consideration, changed the proportion of walls and tower in a manner which should have been counteracted by increasing the height of the western front, including the towers which form a part of it, and the amended drawings comprehended this alteration as an æsthetic necessity, but the increase of height not being a constructional necessity, and the additional cost being of some importance, the full completion of the design was, to the regret of all parties, abandoned till some future time." — Richardson's *Description of the Church.* It should be noted that the interior as well as the exterior of Trinity is still incomplete. Many details remained unfinished at the time and have never been perfected ; and it was Richardson's intention that the great piers should be cased in mosaic and not merely painted as they are to-day.

COMPETITIVE DESIGN FOR TRINITY CHURCH, BOSTON.

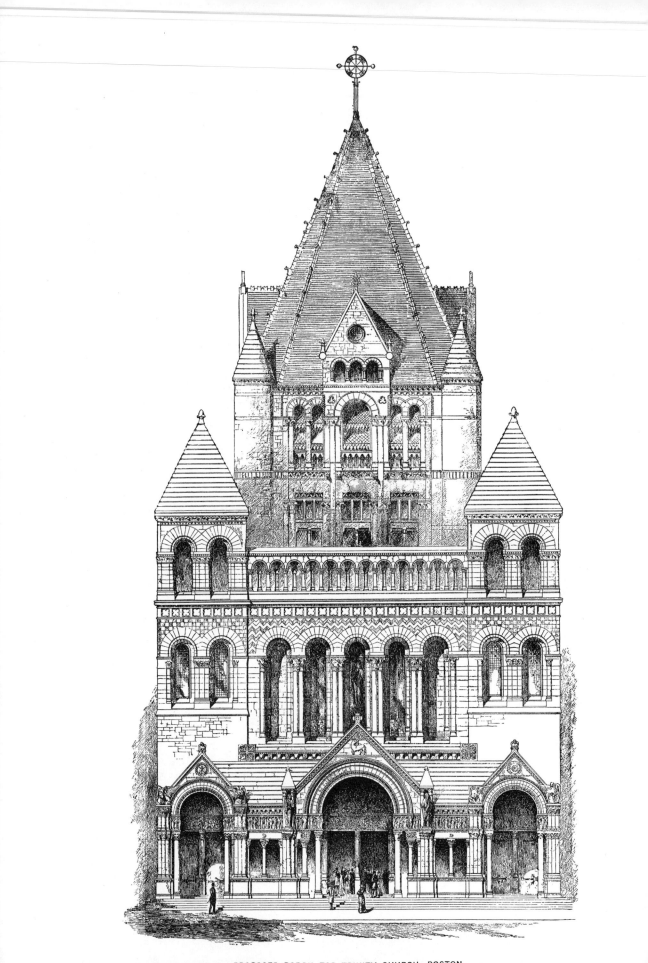

PROPOSED PORCH FOR TRINITY CHURCH, BOSTON.

Brattle Square Church — with two ranges of square mullioned and transomed lights below, and above a very large rose with geometrical bar-tracery. Certain minor features with a complexity of short profiles and steep roof-lines are rather awkwardly added to the south face of the southwestern tower; and the mass which stands between the south transept and the chancel is lower, much less simple, dignified, and harmonious than we see it to-day. The features that adjoin the cloister and the chancel are also much less happily treated, especially as regards their roofs; and all the roofs are shaded in horizontal bands to indicate parti-colored slating. Even the main masses of the church itself were not left unaltered, for in deference to real or supposed acoustic needs, the height of the nave was lessened. The chapel-building was also conspicuously altered, while the cloister-walk was lightened by heightening the columns and simplified by substituting single for coupled shafts. In short, changes were worked in every part and feature of the composition, and in every instance (except as regards the lowering of the nave) were very fortunately worked, resulting in greater simplicity of both conception and treatment, and in completer harmony and unity.

But the greatest change and the happiest was made in the tower, the competition-drawing for which would never be recognized as prepared for Trinity. It shows a tower with a single rectangular stage pierced by three square mullioned and transomed lights in either face, finished with an open parapet, and flanked by angle-turrets, three of which are fluted and go no higher than the parapet, while the one which holds the stair is carried somewhat higher and has a polygonal cap. From this stage rises a tall lantern, much less in diameter and octagonal in shape, with a range of dormers around its base, a large round-arched window with louvre-boards in each face, then a range of narrow rectangular lights with a central column in each, a boldly projecting corbeled cornice with large gargoyles, and an open parapet behind which rises a steep octagonal roof or low steeple. It is an interesting tower in its way, but shows neither conspicuous beauty of feature nor that vital unity between all features which would mark it as a true architectural conception. And, together with many minor features below, it gives the building a semi-Gothic air that does not match at all with our present idea of " Richardsonian " work.

It was always a pleasure to Richardson to look at these drawings — not because he thought them good but because he thought the actual church so much better. After discussing them he once exclaimed: " I really don't see why the Trinity people liked them, or, if they liked them, why they let me do what I afterwards did." Of course the words were whimsically exaggerated, yet they hardly overemphasize the difference between the church as commissioned and the church as built. It seems little less than marvelous that a man should have so developed while a single structure was in progress, and the fact that he did proves how persistent Richardson was in self-criticism and how open to the teaching of new inspirations.

An ever closer study of the Romanesque of southern France gave these inspirations, and its Auvergnese branch is now clearly indicated as that which he preferred. For example, in Trinity we first find him using that bold simple kind of surface - decoration which was a local characteristic of Auvergnese art — that " marquetry-work " in unsculptured stones which was doubtless a survival of the more elaborate and subtile mosaic-work of Gallo-Roman days. Many decorative details still show a mingling of later influences with the Romanesque, while in the chapel-building arched forms are altogether laid aside. In the execution there are also great differences between part and part. Now it is very refined, again almost rude ; now it seems very carefully, again rather carelessly studied. The brain, we feel, was already the brain of a master but the hand was still somewhat immature. The church has a few conspicuous faults and many feeblenesses in detail ; but as a whole it shows, as has well been written, " a remarkable union of richness and breadth, a singular charm of color, and a noble dignity."

A few words more must be given to the tower. In style it harmonizes with the other features, but its prototype is not to be found in Auvergne or in any part of France. Richardson's first design for the tower had never pleased him — had seemed, indeed, so far from right that a fundamentally new conception was what he sought. None had suggested itself up almost to the time when the builders would need definite instruction. But one day when he was ill in bed he was turning over some photographs which had been sent him by his friend La Farge for the sake of the help they might afford in this very problem ; and the instant he saw the tower of the old cathedral at Salamanca he exclaimed, " This is what we want." The suggestion it gave came like a spark to tinder, and a new design was very soon in shape.

If it is instructive to compare this design with the competition-drawing, it is equally so to compare it with the ancient work which was its acknowledged inspiration. We have sometimes been told that Richardson " copied " Trinity's tower from Salamanca's ; and the supposed fact that in this, the first of his great buildings and still the most famous and most popular, he had recourse to a direct process of reproduction, of imitation, has been cited in disproof of his claim to " originality " as an artist.

I think it is hardly necessary to explain that it has never been part of an architect's duty to try to be original in the absolute meaning of the term, or that in these late days of art he could not be so even if he tried his best. A process of intelligent adaptation is that which he must employ, and he has a clear title to be called original whenever he perfectly fits old features to new needs and schemes, or so remoulds an old conception that a new conception is the result — not an effective piece of patch-work but a fresh and vital entity. This last, when we compare the two towers, proves to be what Richardson did when making his so-called copy of Salamanca.

The Salamanca tower has scarcely more than half the diameter of Trinity's and, if one may judge from photographs, is taller in proportion ; and it is polygonal on plan in preparation for a vault of sixteen compartments. Its upper and lower stages are more nearly of the same height than Trinity's, and the lower like the upper bears a round-arched arcade. Its roof is different — taller yet less steep (owing to the considerable entasis that has been given the profile), with the angle faces less conspicuously subordinated to the cardinal faces, and with heavier crockets. Its turrets are proportionately much larger than Trinity's, and all are round and pierced with rows of tall slender lights in both stages, whereas three of Trinity's are round and solid and conically capped while one is round below with staircase slits and above is polygonal with a corresponding cap and a succession of tall round-headed openings. Richardson's gables are more like their prototypes but still are not the same; and even in the second stage of wall-curtain, where the arcade recalls Salamanca more nearly than do the square windows of the lower stage, we find coupled lateral lights instead of single ones.

Nor is there less originality in the treatment than in the choice of his motives. His attached columns are differently grouped, and his introduction of shafts which rise from the base of the tower to the string-course is a novelty — and an important novelty as supplying a flavor of vertical accentuation which wholly lacks at Salamanca. Moreover, the elaborate mouldings of Salamanca are nowhere reproduced; the simple square section used for the arches in the body of Trinity is retained for the tower arches too. In short, not a single feature or detail has been bodily transferred. Great as is the fundamental likeness between the two towers, Richardson imitated the work that inspired him in no closer way than this: He took a general scheme consisting of a massive two-storied body, flanked by angle-turrets and crowned with four gables and an octagonal roof, and then worked out the idea with entire independence alike in the choice and proportioning of his features and in their treatment. There is far less likeness between Trinity and Salamanca than there is between Salamanca and its neighbor at Zamora; yet no historian says more of these than that in one of them must have been found the inspiration for the other. How unjust is the statement that Richardson copied, shows very clearly if we try to compare his work with the old and to decide upon their relative degrees of excellence. We cannot really compare, we can only contrast them. We do not feel that the same ideal was twice conceived and was attained with different degrees of felicity. We feel that different ideals were kept in view. Each result has unity and harmony; but the unity of Salamanca is brought about by a general uniformity in features relieved by minor divergencies in treatment, and the unity of Trinity by a strong opposition of features skillfully worked into vital amalgamation. Clearness, definiteness, is the key-note of the old scheme; mystery — a multifariousness which true artistic feeling has made concordant — is the key-note of the new. The charm of Trinity's tower cannot in the least be appreciated from a picture — noble dignity of scale and a singular beauty of color play too large a rôle. When we are in its presence, it gives us an impression such as modern work rarely produces. It is very rich yet very broad, and is entirely spontaneous and living — distinctly non-mechanical or labored. It looks as though the man who built it had been born to build in just this way; it looks like the result of a genuine impulse and not of a lesson learned and then repeated. In the arrangement and proportioning alike of its forms and of its colors it has that entire felicity which means an air of organic growth — and this is the charm we most rarely find in the cut-and-dried rigidity or the willful yet laborious license of average modern work. It does not become tame and commonplace on long acquaintance, but has that perennial freshness which always marks those results, and only those, that are veritably right and vital. And, as has been said, it dignifies and does not suppress the remainder of the church. Its beauty is greater than that of any other part, but all other parts are consonant in feeling though less refined in treatment — showing more immaturity of thought and hand and giving less evidence of thorough study.

The most serious charge that has been brought against this tower relates to truthfulness of expression — not to that mere beauty of effect which we have thus far considered. Salamanca's tower, it has been said, covers a dome and is exquisitely truthful in design. Trinity's covers a flat ceiling, and, therefore, Richardson's borrowing of Salamanca's form was a lapse from that clear expression of structure which is counted chief among architectural virtues.

There may be a measure of justice in the charge. And yet it is perhaps open to question whether the tower would seem at all untruthful to an observer who had not Salamanca in his mind, who judged it by its own expression only. Of course in the earlier structure the turrets and gables serve as counterpoises to the thrust of the vault. But the alteration of the plan and the lessened size of the turrets alike weaken testimony as to the existence of a vault in Trinity, as do the sharper outline of the roof and the different proportioning of its faces, and the treatment of the upper arcade with its louvre-boards. Examining this tower in and for itself, I think one might perceive the exact truth, — that a flat ceiling comes at the level of the strongly emphasized string-course, above the glazed, below the boarded windows ; and might find the turrets none too massive for the mere supporting to the eye of walls pierced by such a continuity of openings.

Richardson felt, of course, that the porch of Trinity ought to be its most beautiful and elaborate feature — that here should be concentrated a wealth of decoration which would make a harmonious contrast with the masculine severity of the adjacent walls. He never seemed to regret that he had not built it at the same time that he built the rest, knowing that with each subsequent year he had grown in power and skill, especially as regarded the management of ornamental motives. But it was one of his most eager hopes that he might some day be permitted to construct it. Ideas for it were always being turned over in his mind ; more than once they were put on paper ; and after his return from Europe a design was made, so careful, clear, and beautiful that one must hope soon to see it executed. It is based upon the design of that wonderful porch of St. Trophime at Arles, his profound admiration for which has been referred to in a previous chapter, and shows a porch which would extend across the whole breadth of the façade and be some thirty feet in depth. Its multitudinous details would still have received long and patient study had Richardson's life been spared ; but its lines and masses, great and small, are all in place, and as a general scheme he often declared it the final solution of the problem he had so long been considering. The architectural body is conceived so that another hand may easily build it ; and the decorative integument is sufficiently well indicated for a hand trained in Richardson's school to develop it in accordance with his intent.[1]

---

[1] In Appendix IV. will be found some additional extracts from Richardson's description of his church which give an insight into the constructive methods he employed.

WINN MEMORIAL LIBRARY, WOBURN.

CHAPTER XI.

WORKS OF MIDDLE LIFE.

A GLIMPSE OF NORTH EASTON.

THE Cheney Building in Hartford was the first, with the exception of a single dwelling-house, that Richardson designed after Trinity Church had been begun. It was commissioned three years later than Trinity, in September, 1875. It is a large commercial structure, built throughout of Longmeadow sandstone, which has variously arcaded stories, angle pavilions, only one of which rises above the cornice line, and much richness of detail. The scheme is conceived with less individuality than later schemes of a similar kind, and is rather awkwardly managed as regards one or two minor features. Yet it is a scheme which we instinctively judge as a whole and find vigorous, vital, and imposing; and in general its treatment is so skillful that we are tempted to forget how entirely novel at that time was the effort to adapt such a design to such a purpose.

We are likewise impelled to judge the Winn Memorial Library at Woburn, near Boston, commissioned in competition in March, 1877, by contrast not with the contemporary efforts of other hands, but with Richardson's own later works. The first of those public libraries for small towns which are so conspicuous among his best products, it is one of the largest and most complex, and is the most elaborate and picturesque. Its total length is one hundred and sixty-three feet. The main portion contains the reading-room and book-room with subordinate apartments above, and a picture gallery; the octagon is an art-museum.

The first impression the building produces is very powerful and delightful, and its florid picturesqueness has made it very popular with uncritical observers. But it can hardly be called so mature a work as even the Cheney Building. The octagon, though thoroughly pleasing in itself, does not group well with the gable, and is so separated from the library proper that the effect is of two buildings in contact rather than of one building of two parts. In the main portion the grouping lacks simplicity and breadth; there is no dominant centre of interest, and the relationship between feature and feature seems fortuitous, not inevitable. The portal is not satisfactory and is hardly important enough to suit the character of the building, while the tower is too important and is not very felicitous on plan. And a simpler general scheme would have been more appropriate at Woburn. The intense surprise one feels on first coming upon this library through the wide, quiet, grass-bordered streets and among the wooden houses of a small New England town is in part a measure of its beauty, but in part a measure of its unfitness to its place. With all its faults it is a superb building — a strong, fresh, and spontaneous if not a thoroughly organic composition, delightfully elaborated in many of its parts. But when a building is superb in such a way that one's first thought is, What a pity it stands *here*, it is robbed of half its claim, not to admiration, perhaps, but to approbation.

PROPOSED ADDITION TO CHENEY BUILDING, HARTFORD.[1]

One experiment, however, was enough to show Richardson his mistake. In the North Easton library, which was commissioned only six months later, the design is much simpler, soberer, and more organic. Except that there is no octagon, the main features are the same, but their grouping is vastly better. The entrance has due dignity, and its union with the gable gives a true centre of interest. The tower is in good proportion with the lower masses and is well connected with them. The roof is admirably broad and simple. Richness is not excessive and is artistically concentrated upon a few features supported by dignified and quiet fields of wall.

The somewhat crude and over-bold treatment of wall-surfaces which marked much of Richardson's early work had by this time disappeared. But he had not degenerated into technical feebleness or monotony. An interesting surface, and one of a kind to suit the character of the special building he had in hand, was always a chief concern with him. Scale was carefully considered in regulating the average size of the stones, and they were varied among themselves in size and shape with a keen feeling for that degree of difference which should mean animation without restlessness, breadth combined with vitality. The work of the mason was as important in Richardson's eyes as the work of the sculptor; and many a piece of plain wall was pulled down by his orders and rebuilt because

---

[1] As this addition to the Cheney Building was to have been constructed of brick, a wholly different and much more elaborate treatment was adopted than in the main structure; and the illustration in no way suggests the character of this. The management of the large shop-window is the most noteworthy point in the proposed work.

DOORWAY OF LIBRARY, NORTH EASTON.

the desired effect had in some particular been missed. The result justified and more than justified his care, though perhaps few observers pause to appreciate how much it contributes to the general result which they admire.

The interior of the library, including the barrel-vault which covers the long stack-room, is finished in butternut, with delicate carved and turned decoration. Neither inside nor out is the building one of Richardson's very best; yet it approaches the best in excellence, and its entrance-porch is one of the most characteristic he designed.

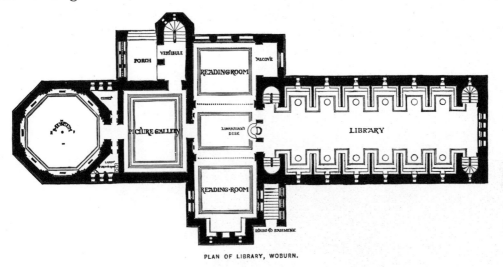

PLAN OF LIBRARY, WOBURN.

Sever Hall, commissioned in October, 1878, was the first work Richardson undertook after his partnership with Mr. Gambrill had been dissolved. It measures about one hundred and seventy-six feet by seventy-five feet, and its interior is divided into plainly finished class-rooms and recitation-rooms. It stands in the college Yard amid many neighboring buildings, but is sufficiently removed from them to be well seen, and is shaded by large trees. It is built of red brick, with a sparing use of Longmeadow stone in the foundations and trimmings. The roof is of red tiles, and the ornamentation is not moulded in terra-cotta but carved in brick — an expedient which secures, of course, much greater sharpness and vitality of effect.

Sever Hall was designed at the period when Richardson had just given himself over, heart and soul, to the leadings of southern Romanesque art, and when the exuberant possibilities of this art had recently seduced him somewhat from sobriety. Therefore its singular simplicity and its paucity of pronounced Romanesque features bear strong witness to the development of his feeling for appropriateness as a prime architectural virtue. Many of the college-buildings — and those which both age and excellence most commended to his respect — were plain rectangular structures of red brick, designed in that genuine Georgian style which is so different from the pseudo-Georgian of Queen Victoria's reign. In later years certain showy, would-be Gothic buildings had forced themselves into this sober company. Richardson was wise enough not to disturb it further by erecting an unsymmetrical, "romantic," Romanesque structure, massive in feature and elaborate in detail. Sever Hall does not imitate the old halls, yet it is not so out of keeping with them as to seem discordant. It is much stronger and more beautiful than they are, yet it does not crush them by its presence. As is the case with Trinity Church, size and color play so large a part in the impression it makes that no picture can reproduce its charm. But even a picture can show the beauty of its simple, imposing outlines, of its organic massing and of the arrangement — neither monotonous nor restless — of its many small openings, and the rich effect produced with so little aid from decoration. The doorway is not too much emphasized to suit the character of the building, but is made finely effective by

LIBRARY, NORTH EASTON.

the great roll-mouldings formed of bricks separately cast for the purpose. The roof and chimneys are superb; and the end with its united yet varied ranges of windows is an epitome of architectural excellence.

The walls of Sever Hall are very beautiful in color — a soft, deep red tending towards crimson. The bright red of the tiles contrasts well with them; the slightly different tone of the carvings adds another touch of variety; and the stone trimmings sufficiently relieve the general redness without being too conspicuous. The treatment of the brick-work is as worthy of notice as Richardson's treatment of stone surfaces. The use of well-made common eastern brick instead of pressed-brick, and the bonding with six successive courses of "stretchers" to one of "headers," produce, in place of the usual hard mechanical surface, a mellow, gently accented, and vital surface, interesting and delightful to the eye.

It is impossible, I think, to pick a fault in Sever Hall unless it be with one detail of decoration, — the carved band beneath the cornice is a little "spotty" owing to the wide spacing of its panels. Otherwise every feature is admirable in itself and admirably fitted to its place, and they all work together to produce a building which is as true and organic a conception as any ever built. It has something even higher than unity to recommend it; it has that noblest architectural

TOWN HALL, NORTH EASTON.

quality we call style. And if its style is individual — if it is not one which can readily be fitted with a historic name — it is not on that account less genuine or less beautiful. Richardson afterwards built structures which showed his imaginative, creative power in a still more convincing light — in designing which he was compelled to deal with more difficult and novel problems. But he never built one wherein the given problem was more perfectly solved, or one for which we may more confidently claim the approving voice of all observers. The excellence and beauty of Sever Hall are so striking yet so serious, sensible, uneccentric, and appropriate, that it is impossible to imagine any critic, however opposed to Richardson's ideas and methods as shown in other works, who should deny to this one a place among the most perfect creations of modern architecture.

A Town Hall for North Easton was commissioned about a year and a half later than the library which has been described above. Both were erected by the Ames family for public use and as memorials, respectively, of Oliver and Oakes Ames. They stand near together on a rocky site in the outskirts of the village. The library is of a warm-toned local granite with trimmings of Longmeadow stone. The hall, which measures ninety-seven feet by fifty-one feet, and seventy-four feet to the top of the tower, is built of the same materials in the lower story and above is of red brick with a wooden half-story at one end. In both buildings the main roofs are of red tiles and the tower roofs of stone.

The site would have been called a difficult one by an architect enamored of the commonplace. But Richardson was too distinctly " a romantic " by birth not to be strongly attracted by those natural diversities of surface which, if rightly used, mean architectural individuality as well as pictorial charm in the result ; and with the aid of Mr. Frederick Law Olmsted he utilized their possibilities to the full. A fine retaining-wall runs along the street, and beyond it the ground rises in abrupt and broken stretches. The hall, which stands much higher than the library, is approached by successive platforms and short flights of steps, kept duly inconspicuous and artistically adapted to the inequalities of the rocky surface. A balustraded wall to connect the two structures was contemplated from the first but unfortunately has not yet been built. Nothing could be better than the way in which each building stands. The slighter swells and depressions of the ground beneath the library have been as carefully respected as the bold rocks that support the hall. Nature has been made to help the work of the architect in the only way which can effect a union fertile in true beauty. Her scheme has been accepted as the foundation for his, and all her suggestions have been emphasized yet harmonized by his treatment. The manner in which the tower of the hall rises out of the rock, almost like a natural development, is the finest feature of the building.

If we compare the loggia of this hall with that of the Springfield Court-house we see how great a change had come over Richardson's art within the space of eight years. The arches of the hall are not quite fortunate in shape, and in deciding upon the proportions of the columns Richardson certainly pushed to a far extreme the mediæval belief that no rule but individual preference in an individual case need determine the relative height and diameter of a shaft. But the arcade has a grand effect, however unscholarly it may be; and it grandly expresses its function as bearing the weight of the building upon its shoulders. Here, as is not the case in Springfield, there is vital relationship and dignified accord between loggia and steps. This loggia is a true conception, not an experimental device, and it is treated in a way which is truly characteristic of its builder though not representative of his highest power.

The Ames monument at Sherman, Wyoming Territory, is a granite pyramid which bears on two of its faces medallions of heroic size, executed by St. Gaudens, representing Oliver and Oakes Ames. It stands at the summit of the pass through the Rocky Mountains at a little distance from the line of the Union Pacific Railroad which the brothers built and which was the first to cross the continent. Mr. Olmsted writes of it : —

" I never saw a monument so well befitting its situation or a situation so well befitting the special character of a particular monument. It is not often seen, apparently, except from a considerable distance, being on the peak of a great hill among great hills with a shanty village on the slope near which the train passes. A fellow-passenger told me that he had several times passed it before that and it had caught his eye from a distance but had seemed to him a natural object. Within a few miles there are several conical horns of the same granite projecting above the smooth surface of the hills. It is a most tempestuous place, and at times the monument is under a hot fire of little missiles driven by the wind. But I think they will only improve it." There is no law, it seems, so binding but that it may permit exceptions ; even the imitation of a work of nature may occasionally produce a good result in art.

The Boston Park Commission employed Richardson in April, 1880, to design a bridge for the new Back Bay Basin — a chain of tide-flooded ponds with wide borders of grass and shrubbery. The bridge carries a broad road which will eventually be a closely-built street, and is simply utilitarian in character. But the fine curve of the single great round arch and the charming color of the pudding-stone make it a thing of beauty as well as of very evident strength and serviceableness.

SKETCH FOR A TOWN HALL FOR BROOKLINE.

CHAPTER XII.

THE ALBANY CAPITOL.

RICHARDSON's commission to work on the New York State Capitol at Albany placed him for the only time in his life publicly in opposition to other members of his profession. The story is a very complicated one, involving questions of state finance and party politics and professional etiquette as well as questions of art. Only its main incidents can be noted here, but a prefatory word must be said about the way in which the undertaking was managed.

From the day when the foundations of the Capitol were laid until this, charges of reckless extravagance and scandalous waste in the management of the work have been incessantly made by politicians opposed to those for the time being in power, and all persons holding any position of responsibility in connection with the building have been held up to public odium as faithless public servants. As far as the architects are concerned it should be better known than it seems to be that, in accordance with a most unfortunate system of administration, they were not employed to superintend the work but merely to give counsel in architectural questions and to prepare plans for others to carry out. They had no responsibility for those parts of the undertaking in which, if anywhere, public money was likely to be misused. They determined neither the rates of wages and salaries, nor who should receive them, nor the length of a day's work. The organization and discipline of the great force employed, the purchase of materials, the making of contracts, the keeping of accounts, — all these matters were in other hands, and their own pay was received month by month as a stated salary, not as a commission on the cost of the work. In repeated legislative investigations nothing calculated to throw a suspicion upon the integrity or conscientiousness of any architect who had been employed on the building was discovered. The Capitol cost enormous sums both before and after Messrs. Eidlitz, Richardson, and Olmsted took it in hand. But the way in which it had been begun precluded the possibility of really economical treatment on their part, and though some persons may think that they ought nevertheless to have made their work less costly than they did, the question is one which involves merely their good sense and good taste as artists, not their good faith as public servants.

The new Capitol had been begun in 1868 with the understanding that it was not to cost more than four million dollars.[1] When the Legislature met in 1875 it had cost five millions, and was very far from complete even up to the floor of the third story — the highest point to which the walls had been carried. At least seven millions more were declared needful to complete it in accordance with the

[1] The materials for this summary have been gathered from the newspapers of the time and the published reports of proceedings in the New York Legislature.

designs of the architect in charge, and it was apparent to the most superficial observer that these designs were proving unsatisfactory in almost every practical respect. The Legislature therefore appointed a new Commission, with Lieutenant-Governor Dorsheimer as its chairman, to inquire into the prospects of the work, and resolved to grant no more money except upon its recommendation. This Commission appointed Messrs. Eidlitz, Richardson, and Olmsted as its Advisory Board of Architects.[1] Early in 1878 a detailed report based upon a careful examination of the building itself and of the architect's drawings was submitted by the Board to the Commission and by the Commission to the Senate.

This report explained that the existing work had in general been well done and that the foundations and basement of the building, contrary to public belief, were of " vast strength." It declared the scheme to be full of grave practical defects, explaining them in a lucid way and adding that most of them could not be remedied without rebuilding the entire structure upon a radically different groundplan. The fact that the legislative chambers had been relegated to the third story was named as the most conspicuous mistake, while among the others were dark corridors, rooms now too small for their purpose and now too large, insufficient light, undignified stairways, and inconvenient approaches to the chief apartments. The more purely artistic aspect of the scheme was then discussed at length. The verdict was again severe but again clear reasons for the severity were given.

With this report the Board of Architects submitted, by request, sketches to show how in their opinion the design might be altered for the better. Also by request they soon afterwards submitted full drawings, based on these sketches, for comparison with those of the architect in charge, accompanied by estimates and by tenders from responsible contractors to show how money might be saved by the change.[2]

As soon as the existence and character of these designs were known a storm of opposition broke. No one questioned that the Capitol scheme had been in a deplorable condition or doubted the justice of the special criticisms made by the Advisory Board. But some professional voices asserted that the architect in charge ought first to have been asked to suggest possible improvements, and condemned the Board for having submitted such elaborate drawings even at the Commission's direct request ; and many cried out with emphasis against the character of these designs. The building had been begun in a Roman Renaissance style. Messrs. Eidlitz and Richardson proposed to complete it in a Romanesque style. The intrinsic merits of the two designs were but little discussed. Almost all the protests were chiefly inspired, and many of them were wholly inspired, by indignation at the thought of seeing in a single building a union of two different styles. The newspapers of the entire State soon joined in the battle. Most of them took

---

[1] Mr. Olmsted, although not an architect, was associated in this Board upon equal terms with the two architects because of his practical familiarity with their art and his long experience with large public undertakings.

[2] Volumes i. and ii. of *The American Architect and Building News* contain a condensation of this report, a discussion of the original design, reproductions both of this design and of the one submitted by the Board, and many letters referring to the various questions at issue, including one from the architect in charge. This letter states that the Legislature was itself responsible for the chief faults in his building, having prescribed the position of the legislative chambers and having constantly interfered in his later work.

SOUTH FRONT OF THE CAPITOL, ALBANY.

INTERIOR OF SENATE CHAMBER, CAPITOL, ALBANY.

the part of the Board, translating a public sentiment which cared little for abstract questions of style, much for the chance that in some ways at least the Capitol would profit by a change of architects. The chief professional journal of the
country tried to preserve a safe neutrality. No protests changed the attitude of
the Board; and none disturbed Richardson's peace of mind until in March, 1876, a
formal remonstrance was addressed to the Senate by the New York Chapter of the
American Institute of Architects. Being himself a member of this Chapter, he
thought it should have given him a hearing before it publicly condemned his
course; and he also felt aggrieved by what he considered the discourteous tone of
the document. A draft of a reply exists among his papers, together with a number of letters from well-known architects and professors of art deploring the action
of the Chapter and the similar action of other Chapters which had less right to
interfere in the matter. But Richardson decided not to publish any reply, feeling that the public was with him and that a good part of the profession was not
against him, and believing that works, not words, are the best arguments for an
artist's use.

By order of the Commission work upon the Capitol was resumed in accordance
with the new designs. In March, 1877, however, the outcry against them was
still so strong that a council of five New York architects was summoned before
the Committees of Ways and Means and of Finance to testify " as experts as to
the propriety of the changes made in the plans of the architect for the State Capitol building by the Advisory Board." Their report was again a decided condem-
nation of these changes and again was not very courteous in tone, charging that
the course of the Board in substituting another style amounted to a confession
that its members felt incompetent to manage the style first selected. The matter was referred for decision to the Finance Committee. By a majority report,
against which a minority report protested, it was declared that it had not been
" intended or expected by the Legislature . . . that the style of architecture
should be materially changed," and that the Board's project was " radically defec-
tive not only in design but in the treatment of the material used — granite."
The Legislature thereupon voted one million dollars to carry on the work, subject
to the condition that the first scheme should again be adopted. Governor Rob-
inson vetoed the bill, probably because of this condition. Both houses then passed
over the veto an appropriation of five hundred thousand dollars, but without making any reference to the question of style; and in June the Capitol Commission
instructed the Board to proceed with its work.

The Board was collectively responsible before the public for all parts of the
work; but in execution Richardson and Mr. Eidlitz divided it between them.
The former took charge of the exterior and of the interior of the south side, which
contains the senate chamber; and the latter of the interior of the north side, with
the assembly chamber, and of the great tower which has not yet been built. Only
Richardson's portion of the work can be considered here. The illustration shows
his treatment of the exterior with sufficient clearness. In the two stories below
the roof a pure form of Romanesque has been adhered to, though with many variations from the first design. After these stories had been built on the north side,
the Legislature again decreed a return to a Renaissance style. It was plainly im-

possible to return to that employed in the lower stories, so Richardson did what he could to obey orders by designing his roof and dormers in an Early-Renaissance, " free classic," manner more in harmony with his own arcades. The north and south front are similar in scheme, but differ in the proportioning of their features, as Richardson thought the one first completed somewhat weak in effect.

If the building as it stands is compared with the original design no one can now deny that the State was fortunate in its second choice of architects. Although its lack of unity prevents it from taking rank with the most successful buildings in the country, it is one of the most interesting and impressive. Considered in themselves, its upper portions — despite the discrepancies in style which even there occur — are beautiful in composition as well as in detail. Architectural order has been brought out of the chaos below, and as clear an expression of the interior has been given as the circumstances of the case permitted. In a near view the beauty of these upper portions richly compensates for the lack of unity in general effect ; and in a more distant view they alone are noticeable. Richardson's work, as he foresaw, is the best justification of his course. It is needless now to insist that this course was not dictated by inability to manage a Renaissance scheme or by a mere self-seeking impulse. Yet it is but just to say that those who took pains to inquire into the matter knew at the time as well as every one sees to-day, that he had good reasons to give for his choice of a Romanesque manner of treatment. It was the manner of treatment which in all cases, at this period of his life, he theoretically approved. It had no such claim, however, upon Mr. Eidlitz's preference, as his work in the interior of the Capitol is enough to show ; yet Mr. Eidlitz shared Richardson's wish to adopt it in this case and Mr. Olmsted approved their joint decision because, to the one as to the other, it seemed to offer the best chance for a true expression in the exterior of the internal structure, arrangements, and special services of the different parts of the building. Had the same artists been called upon to complete a building which had been well begun in a Renaissance style, they would certainly not have substituted another style. But it seemed to them that here the question was not between unity and disharmony in style so much as between a wholly bad building and one which might be partly good. And though they knew their course was open to criticism from the modern standpoint, they must have drawn confidence from the countless precedents which the greater ages of their art afford. When mediæval builders set a Lancet-Pointed on top of a Norman story, or a rigid Perpendicular on top of a florid Gothic story, unity of effect was much more conspicuously violated than in the Albany Capitol. It is true that they expressed the tastes and wishes of their whole generation, while Richardson and Eidlitz expressed only their personal convictions with regard to what was best ; but this was as unquestionably to them the right guide to follow.

As the north front was first built, the assembly chamber was opened long before the senate chamber ; and Mr. Eidlitz's two staircases were soon finished, while Richardson's larger one has not yet risen above the first story. His great library also has barely been begun, but as he left full drawings for it we may hope for its completion at no distant date.

The senate chamber was opened in March, 1881. Its dimensions as at first

FIRE-PLACE IN COURT OF APPEALS ROOM. CAPITOL, ALBANY

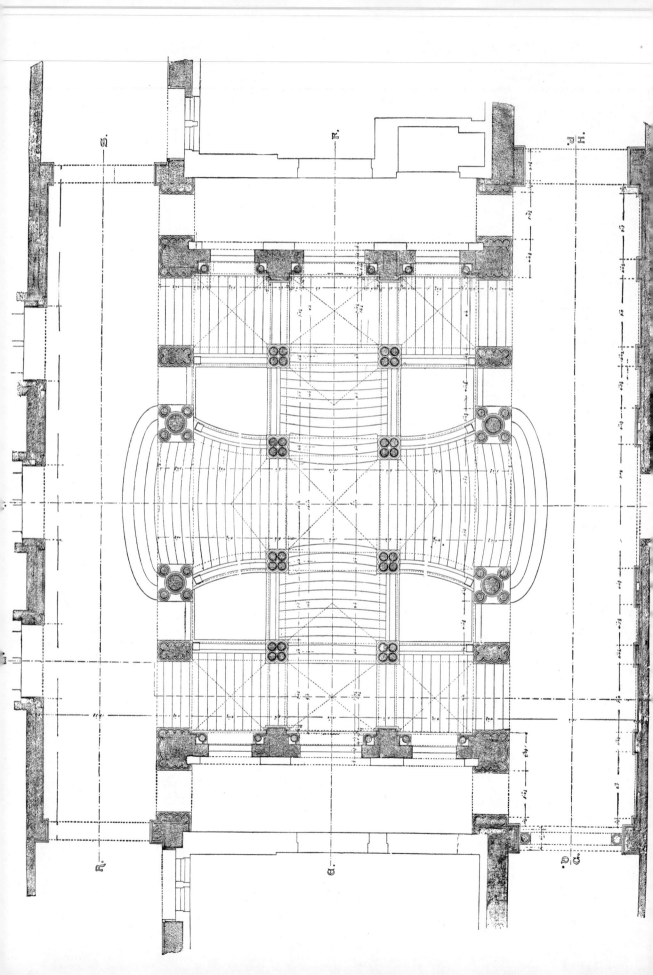

established could not be changed by Richardson; but they were so much greater than was desirable — allowing nearly one hundred feet by sixty feet for the accommodation of only thirty-two senators — that he reduced them by treating the ends as lobbies, divided off by massive arcades, and placing the visitors' galleries above them. Beauty as well as convenience is greatly increased by these arcades; they redeem to the eye the existence of two superimposed ranges of windows — another relic of the original design that could not be done away with; and the individuality which they give to the room is so thoroughly architectural in character that its rich materials and lavish decorations play a properly subordinate part in the impression it produces.[1] The lower walls, as far up as the spring of of the arches of the first range of windows, are faced with reddish-gray Knoxville granite, smoothly finished but not polished. Above this for a space of about twelve feet they are covered with polished panels of mottled, semi-translucent Mexican onyx framed in bands of yellow Sienna marble. Above this paneling is a simple marble string-course, and the upper walls are covered with gilded leather. The columns are of dark red-brown granite, the capitals of whitish marble, and the arches of Sienna marble. The galleries, which are bowed between the columns into slightly projecting balconies, have balusters of Sienna marble and gray marble rails. The oaken beams of the ceiling are four feet in depth — not an excessive size for a room fifty feet in height — and, like the panels between them, are richly carved and touched with color. The great chimney-breasts have not yet been carved, nor are all the sculptured details in other parts of the room complete or all the windows filled with suitable glass. The furniture is of mahogany and red leather. In its color effect, as in its architectural scheme, the room is one of the most superbly successful and one of the most individual that has been built in modern times. Its acoustic properties are excellent.

Among the other apartments which Richardson completed are the governor's room and the court of appeals room. The latter is less striking in effect than the senate chamber, but hardly less beautiful; and it would be as perfect in treatment had the great stone window-arches been supported by pilasters of the same material. The red-oak paneling which covers the walls has been used for the jambs as well, somewhat to the detriment of solidity of effect. On the long wall opposite the windows it is so disposed as to frame a row of historic portraits. Its details are everywhere profuse but delicate in treatment and quiet in effect. The screen in front of the judges' platform is particularly rich yet refined in motive, and the vast marble mantel is the most beautiful, perhaps, that Richardson designed.

The design for the great staircase was perfected in Richardson's later years, and when complete it will be one of the finest features of the building. The well in which it rises measures about seventy feet square, and the material is a pale red Scotch sandstone.

---

[1] These are the arches which the English historian and critic Freeman praised by a comparison which to him meant more than any other — by saying that in general conception they were " worthy to stand at Ragusa." And it was the Romanesque work on the Capitol as a whole which convinced him that this style was the best for American use. No praise which Richardson ever received pleased him so much as this.

CHAPTER XIII.

WORKS OF MIDDLE LIFE.

CITY HALL, ALBANY.

RICHARDSON's five library buildings afford an excellent chance to trace the development of his talent. Two have already been described. The third was the Crane Memorial Library for Quincy, Mass., commissioned in May, 1880. The two others — the Billings Library for the University of Vermont at Burlington, and the Converse Memorial Library at Malden, near Boston — were not commissioned until three years later but may best be considered here. At Quincy and at Burlington Richardson reached the most perfect expression of the general scheme upon which all five are based.

The Quincy building bears the nearest analogy to that at North Easton, but is still better as regards appropriateness of effect and architectural coherence and charm. The book-room wing is practically the same. But the insertion in the front of the great window which lights the reading-room, the lowering of the gable and diminution of its arcade, the alteration into a staircase turret of the tower, which at North Easton is too authoritative in expression to suit the purpose and surroundings of the building, and its more vital uniting with the façade, the extension of the line of the roof in an unbroken sweep, and the enlivening of its slope by the useful lit-

WINDOW IN GABLE OF LIBRARY, QUINCY.

tle windows — all these changes are expressionally fortunate ; and the compacter massing which results from them is as fortunate from a purely æsthetic point of view. Here at last is a whole in which all parts are so fused together that it is impossible to disassociate them in thought. The building looks as though it had been conceived at a single inspiration, born by a single impulse. But this means of course that it

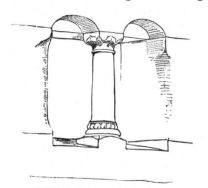

WINDOW IN PORCH OF LIBRARY, QUINCY.

was the result of patient constructive thought, of well-trained reasoning skill. Inside, the plan is excellent and the treatment very beautiful. Largely in answer to Richardson's own needs and as a result of the difficult yet rational tasks he set and the exacting criticism he applied to their execution, a school of wood-

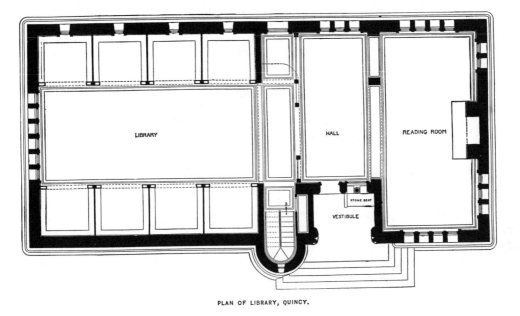

PLAN OF LIBRARY, QUINCY.

carvers had by this time been developed which was capable of doing work at once vigorous and refined, spirited and delicate. He furnished the designs for such work from his own office, where they were as carefully elaborated as his exterior decorations; and in Mr. Evans's workshop in Boston they were carried out as

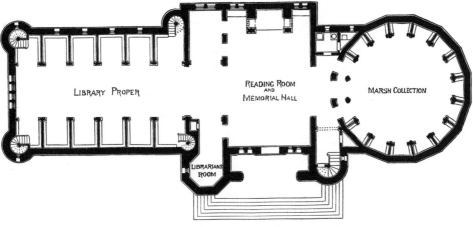

PLAN OF LIBRARY, BURLINGTON.

few designs have been in recent times. The interior of the Quincy Library is a rich example. The many slender pilasters are delicately reeded, and their capitals constantly vary in motive. The little cornices are exquisite, and the great chimney-breast with its Byzantinesque decoration, largely based upon suggestions afforded by native plants, is a remarkable piece of truly architectural ornament. The carving is everywhere abundant but nowhere sins by over-abundance; and the grace and spirit of the execution lead one to examine it with a care more often given to ancient than to modern work. It is a convincing answer to those critics who have said that the Romanesque motives which Richardson preferred lack those qualities of refinement, balance, harmony, and grace which since the days of the classic Renaissance modern taste demands. Richardson's decoration

SKETCH FOR LIBRARY, BURLINGTON.

sometimes erred on the side of over-boldness, barbaric luxuriance, diversity, and emphasis. But when, as in this Quincy interior, he based his work upon those Byzantine developments the likeness of which to classic developments is so clear and close, he proved the entire fitness of Romanesque art to meet the most refined demands of modern taste. And in the harmonious interpolation of motives taken directly from neighboring woods and fields he proved the possibilities for further development which the style possesses.

LIBRARY, BURLINGTON.

In the Billings Library at Burlington, commissioned in 1883 and finished shortly before Richardson's death, the exterior features are similar to those employed at Woburn though the plan is different and the polygon has another use. How great is again the improvement upon the first expression of the idea! Woburn is a striking assemblage of picturesquely connected but not integrally united parts; Burlington, though combined of as many parts, is a true, a homogenous whole. Perhaps it is not so striking but it has truer dignity. It is at once more simple and more beautiful. For a University library standing among other large

CRANE MEMORIAL LIBRARY, QUINCY.

CITY HALL, ALBANY.

buildings the tower is not too important; and if the stack-room wing seems a little too short, it should be noted that an additional bay, contemplated in Richardson's design, was omitted in the execution from motives of economy. The dimensions of the two buildings are the same within a very few feet; but while Woburn shows an intermingling of granite and sandstone, Burlington is built entirely of sandstone. The interior is finished in hard pine and the polygon is covered with an open timber roof. The walls are simply decorated in water-color.

SKETCH FOR READING ROOM, LIBRARY, BURLINGTON.

I once heard Richardson say that when he built Woburn he was in his "pyrotechnic stage." Any of his later works might serve to show the difference between that stage and the one in which he expressed his mature development, yet in no way could it have been so clearly shown as by the chance which Burlington offered him to build, as it were, the same library over again.

The Malden library, as our illustration shows, differs from the others in the arrangement of its plan. It is a picturesque, individual, and excellent piece of work, but it has neither the dignity of Burlington nor the wholly satisfying charm of Quincy. Another illustration shows the autographic first sketch for the plan of a large library on a lot of unusual shape. It was made in May, 1884, and afterwards elaborated for a competition in which Richardson was unsuccessful.

We may now return to our chronological notice of his works of other kinds. Eight months later than the commission for the Quincy Library came, in competition, the commission to build a City Hall at Albany, N. Y. The site had been fortunately selected. The great State Capitol stands on top of a high steep hill from which the streets run down to the older portion of the town. The old State House had stood just below it, on a sort of broad plateau which interrupts the declivity; and on the opposite side of this plateau, where the descent begins again,

SKETCH FOR BOOK ROOM, LIBRARY, BURLINGTON.

the new City Hall was placed. Thus it dominates the city, and is dominated in its turn by the greater building which represents the greater authority of the Commonwealth.

It is unnecessary to say much more about the City Hall than our illustrations tell. It is admirably adapted to the irregularities of the ground, and the combination with the jail in the rear is cleverly effected — a covered bridge bringing the prisoners directly from their cells into the court-rooms in the main structure. The great porch with the loggia above is a characteristic piece of composition; and the concentration of ornament here and upon the gable and the upper part of the tower relieves without disturbing the massive simplicity of the other portions. The enormous tower appropriately expresses civic authority; and it has a novel

STUDY FOR REAR OF CITY HALL, ALBANY.

practical use as a conveniently arranged storehouse for the city's historic papers. In design it is a very free adaptation of southwestern Romanesque precedents. Or, more truly, it is a bold development of these precedents along a new and individual line. There may be a difference of opinion as to the wisdom of using

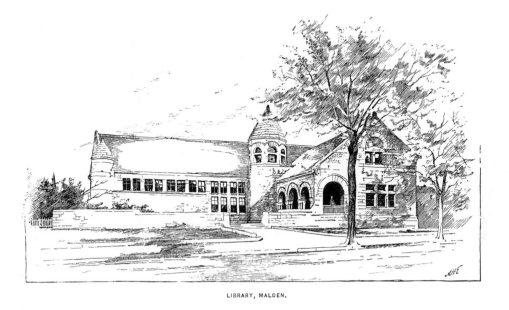

LIBRARY, MALDEN.

unrelieved light stone in its lower and unrelieved dark stone in its upper portions. But there can be none as to the fine simplicity and reticence of all the lower portions, or as to the vigorous beauty of the outline of the tower. One important factor in the effect of this, however, cannot be appreciated in a picture — the bold batter which sets the great body so firmly and gracefully on its feet. A comparison of this tower with that of the Brattle Square Church strikingly shows the change which had come over Richardson's attitude toward Romanesque art as a quarry of elements for the modern designer's use.

Austin Hall — a Law School building for Harvard University — was commissioned in February, 1881. It measures two hundred and sixteen feet in length, and was built at a cost of about one hundred and forty-five thousand dollars. In outline and massing it is simple almost to severity, and the symmetry and solidity of

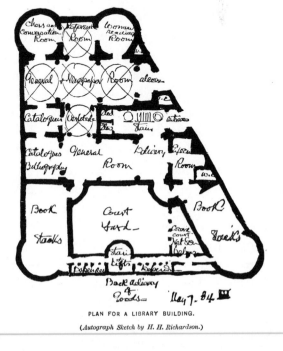

PLAN FOR A LIBRARY BUILDING.

(*Autograph Sketch by H. H. Richardson.*)

the wings and the quietness of the gray slated roof well sustain the richness of the central façade and the striking color of the walls.

Richardson here departed from his usual method of constructing with sandstone alone or with a light-toned granite trimmed with sandstone. The ashlar is of dark Longmeadow sandstone, the trimmings are of pale yellow Ohio stone, and blue-stone is introduced in the mosaic patterns. A fortunate result is not often secured by a color scheme which takes a conspicuously lighter tone for the most emphatic members; but it is unusually satisfactory here, as the large relative quantity and the good disposition of the Ohio stone prevent any look of weakness or confusion. It is certain that at this period of his life Richardson would not have used so striking a color scheme in any building less austerely composed than

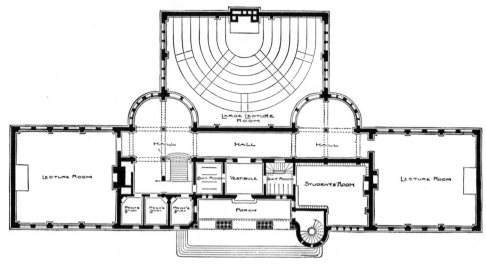

PLAN OF LAW SCHOOL, HARVARD UNIVERSITY.

the Law School; but it may be questioned whether, even as it is, the effect is not a little too striking. Yet it is very beautiful and lacks neither dignity nor coherence. Quite possibly it is merely the neighborhood of Sever Hall which tempts one to think the front of the Law School a little overdone, while no piece of work that Richardson ever executed exceeds the back of this building for purely architectural beauty — for the virtues of good proportion, harmonious outlines, well-arranged features, artistic treatment of surfaces, and simple dignity of expression.

The interior of the School was very carefully planned, and except that the vestibule and the longitudinal hall are not quite commodious enough, it is very successful. The finish throughout is plain but dignified. The walls are wainscoted and plastered. The massive radiating arches of brick which spring from the columns in the two rectangular halls are square in section, but furnished with a deeply undercut roll at either edge. The responds are also of brick, but the low sturdy columns are of polished granite with heavy carved capitals of Knoxville marble. The stairways sin, if at all, by too great simplicity. The large reading-room over the lecture-amphitheatre is beautifully proportioned, well lighted and suitably furnished. The coved and paneled ceiling is supported by great tie-beams borne on long corbels. The immense fire-place and chimney-breast are of brick and Ohio stone. There is no mantel, but a broad slab above the fire-place bears a Latin inscription in honor of Samuel Austin, to whose memory the School

PORCH OF LAW SCHOOL, HARVARD UNIVERSITY.

was built by his brother; and over this is a charmingly decorated cornice supported by vast foliated brackets — conventionalized representations of gnarled apple-branches.

For nearly seven years after the Cheney Building in Hartford was built Richardson had no occasion to design a large commercial warehouse. But in March, 1882, Mr. Frederick L. Ames gave him the commission to build one at Bedford and Kingston streets in Boston. It is a costly and monumental work, entirely of Longmeadow stone, occupying a broadly rounded corner site. Although it cannot be entirely seen from any point of view, at the first glance it is extremely impressive; and the longer one looks the more imposing it appears as a whole, while features of the greatest merit reveal themselves in the design. The successive ranges of arcaded openings are beautifully proportioned, and the fact that each of the lower ones embraces two stories of the interior is frankly indicated in their construction. The size of the dormers does not seem as unduly great as the photograph leads one to believe; and the unconventional way in which they break

EMMANUEL CHURCH, ALLEGHENY CITY.

through the cornice is not displeasing to the eye. A keen feeling for appropriateness of expression is shown by the small size and inconspicuous character of the doorways; — dearly as Richardson loved a great arched portal, he knew when it would be out of place and when the windows should be more important. The details of decoration are carefully studied throughout, and nothing more beautiful was ever designed in the Brookline office than the strong, rich, yet delicate coupled lights of the upper arcade. But despite the beauty of the building and the excellence of many of its parts, this store can hardly be called one of Richardson's most satisfactory productions. As a monument pure and simple it is superb; as a building adapted to commercial uses it has the defect of inappropriateness. When we examine the design part by part and consider for what service it was intended, this service does, indeed, make itself clearly manifest; — no building with a lower story of this pattern and with so constant a succession of uniform openings above could have been meant for any other use. It is the richness of the execution which is inappropriate. We have so few superb monuments in our cities that we can hardly be conscientious enough to regret that this one is so superb. But as the adequate expression of the given problem in its entirety, — and in consequence as an example for others, a type, a model, — it cannot be as highly valued as some of Richardson's other buildings. For his own sake, and especially for the sake of his influence upon American art, it was well that he lived long enough to solve the same problem again in a more perfect way.

The summer of this year Richardson spent, as has been told, in Europe. The months next after his return he devoted to the competition-drawings for the Albany Cathedral.

SKETCH FOR A CHAPEL.

AMES BUILDING, BOSTON.

CHAPTER XIV.

THE CATHEDRAL DRAWINGS. — THE PITTSBURGH COURT-HOUSE.

CATHEDRAL CHURCH.
(Autograph Sketch by H. H. Richardson.)

WHILE still in Europe Richardson had agreed to compete for the commission to build a Protestant Episcopal cathedral church at Albany. It was not until the latter part of October, however, that he could give the scheme serious attention, and it was almost the end of November before he got fairly to work on the drawings. About four months later they were finished. The time seems short when we see their elaborate perfection. They are very large in size and nine in number, including plan, perspective, exterior and interior elevations, longitudinal and transverse sections, and a sheet of details upon which even the subjects for the stained-glass windows are fully indicated. Their interest would be very great if they merely showed the high degree of technical skill which Richardson's pupils had acquired. In no office in the world could a more clear, complete, and beautifully executed set of drawings be prepared. More than two of them would have been published with this volume had it proved possible in reducing them to preserve their beauty or even their significance.

The instructions laid before the competing architects described a site which measured two hundred and eighty-six feet by one hundred and forty feet, and a soil of stratified clay which would require the greatest care in preparing the foundations. The cathedral was to be Gothic in style, to follow " to some extent the traditional arrangements of the Church," and to seat from fifteen hundred to eighteen hundred persons on the ground floor. The choir was to be furnished with stationary seats but the nave to be left free for the use of chairs. In addition to the church itself there were required: A bishop's vestry with treasury attached; other vestries for clergy and choir; a chapter-house; a hall to accommodate one hundred persons, and a covered bridge to connect the north side of the church with a school across the street. It was also prescribed that, as it was probable that the whole of the structure could not be immediately built, the architect should show how a portion of the expenditure might be postponed, either by deferring the execution of part of the constructive work or by deferring only the ornamental work and " erecting the structural parts complete or in such manner as may be considered desirable by the architect, bearing in mind that the works of the first stage must provide a building fit and proper for occupation by the whole number of persons mentioned." Two separate drawings of the building as it would be in this first stage were required, and a limit of one hundred and fifty thousand dollars was set as its total cost. No limit of cost was set with regard to the completed cathedral.

The proposed site seemed to Richardson too small, but he was told it could not be enlarged. The reduction of his plan will show the main arrangements of his church, which, as his accompanying memoranda explained, he tried " to avoid making merely an enlarged parish church." All the accessory apartments are supplied on the ground level except the treasury, which is placed in the crypt under the bishop's vestry ; and, in addition, a baptistry is supplied beneath the northwestern turret, and the hall is so treated as to be useful for chapel-services. The design well illustrates one of Richardson's greatest merits — his power to appreciate the value both of ancient forms consecrated by persisting sentiment and of practical modern needs, and to put the one without violence to the service of the other. It follows " the traditions of the Church " not merely " to some extent," but as they are represented in fully developed mediæval examples. Yet when we examine it we find that no mediæval feature has been kept simply for the sake of correctness ; each has its use, traditional whenever possible, novel whenever necessary, but when novel none the less appropriate. For example, no ecclesiastical features are more beautiful in exterior or in interior effect than the ambulatories and apsidal chapels of great French churches, and none are more helpful in accenting the difference between a mere parish church and something nobler. We have no saints to-day whom we worship behind the high-altar at altars of their own ; but Richardson was surely wise to preserve the form of their sanctuaries when providing the several vestries that were required of him. He was also wise to meet our modern wish for comfort by surrounding a great part of his church with wide, low, vaulted passages or lobbies, especially as they give additional beauty to both the interior and the exterior perspectives, and in no way detract from the scholarly correctness of his scheme as a whole.

When we turn to the other drawings we see that he interpreted in a very liberal way the prescription that the church should be " Gothic in style." His main arches are slightly pointed, but nowhere else has he varied from the precedents of pure Romanesque art. As a consequence, no design could be less Gothic in effect or feeling, as a whole or in detail. Only by a straining of terms can we say even so much as that it is in a Transitional style. It is so clearly, so emphatically Romanesque that we feel it would hardly be more purely Romanesque were all its arches semi-circles. Even so optimistic a man as Richardson must have known that in presenting such a scheme he seriously compromised his chances of success. Doubtless he not only hoped but believed, either that his faint semblance of a surrender to their wishes would satisfy his judges or else that the intrinsic beauty of his design would revolutionize those wishes. But be this as it may, he could not have consented, at any time in his maturer years, to build a really Gothic church, and least of all at this particular time when he was fresh from the study of ancient Romanesque art and more than ever convinced of its peculiar fitness for modern adaptation. A man of a different mould might have thought that the holding of such beliefs forbade him to enter this competition. But Richardson believed that the first duty of an artist was the eager use of every possible

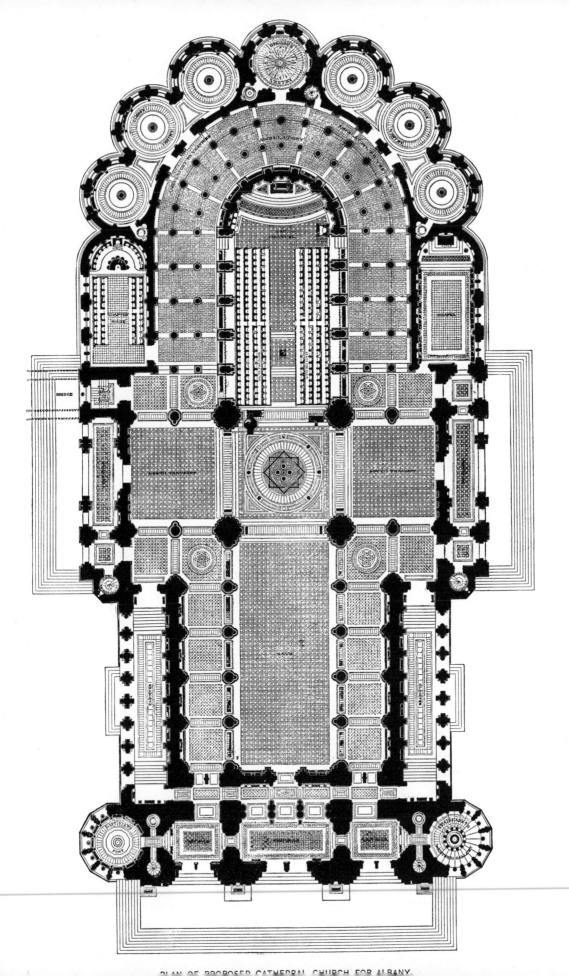

PLAN OF PROPOSED CATHEDRAL CHURCH FOR ALBANY.

PERSPECTIVE VIEW OF PROPOSED CATHEDRAL CHURCH FOR ALBANY.

ELEVATION OF PROPOSED CATHEDRAL CHURCH FOR ALBANY.

opportunity to impose his own ideas of art upon the world. As will be seen from his memoranda,[1] he pointed out to the committee how his design might be altered to make it less expensive ; but he never hinted at any possibility of alteration in the matter of style. And in after days when he spoke of the chance he had lost, it was always to regret that he had not been allowed to build the church in his own way — never that he had not tried harder to persuade himself to build it in another's way.

Only a careful study of all the drawings in their original size can show how perfectly Richardson had absorbed the very marrow and spirit of his chosen style. It is impossible to point to any one ancient church which is the plain prototype of this. But I think it would be impossible to find any which more perfectly represents the highest possibilities of the style it follows except as size is an element in grandeur of effect ; and none is a more vital entity, a more organic whole. Those who know the precedents upon which he drew are astonished at the scholarliness of Richardson's treatment ; but those who do not know them feel its logical and vital excellence as strongly. We may like his design or not, but we like it or dislike it as a whole, and according to our personal taste in the matter of style. We do not say that it is better in one part than in another, more beautiful here than there. As has been already explained, we cannot regret that Richardson was forced to spend his few remaining years upon work of a different sort. Yet nothing could have been more fortunate for his fame than that he should have prepared these drawings. While they reveal a side of his endowment which without them we should never have appreciated, they throw the brightest light upon the principles which ruled his practice as a whole. They show that he had a scholarly grasp upon the richest traditional resources of his art which the most purely antiquarian of architects might envy, and therefore they prove that

GRANITE CAPITAL, COURT-HOUSE, PITTSBURGH.

when he was not scholarly it was of deliberate intent, that when, in the maturity of his power, he was "free" or "eclectic" in treatment, it was because he felt that fitness did not call for historic accuracy, that practical or expressional needs demanded more of inventive and less of reproductive effort. Some explanatory extracts from the memoranda he submitted with his drawings are given in an appendix. Further analysis of them would be useless, as it cannot be accompanied by the whole series in illustration.[2]

Richardson's success in the competition for the county buildings at Pittsburgh, Pa., was announced in February, 1884. The contracts fixed the cost of the work

---

[1] See Appendix IV.

[2] The legacy Richardson has left us in these drawings is too precious to be lost. If in any part of America another cathedral church is desired their existence should surely be remembered.

at $2,243,024. It has been finished since Richardson's death. The site was fortunately chosen, on top of the highest hill in a hilly town.

The main building, which forms a hollow square, measures three hundred and one feet by two hundred and nine feet, and in the rear, connected with it by a covered bridge, stands the jail. The court-yard within the main building measures one hundred and forty-five feet by seventy feet, is entered by two great arched passage-ways, and may conveniently be used as a place for public meetings. In its principal features the plan of the building is the same on all the floors excepting as regards the great staircase, which is of two flights only, beginning in the basement and leading to the great halls of the first and second stories. Four other large staircases and four elevators are accommodated in tow-

GRANITE CAPITAL, COURT-HOUSE, PITTSBURGH.

ers at the angles of the court-yard, and rise to the top of the building. All the rooms lie on the outside of the wings towards the street, and are connected by corridors which encircle the court-yard. The first story is twenty-five feet, the second twenty-nine feet high in the large apartments; but in the smaller ones this height is divided to admit of half-stories or mezzanines. The small rooms are thus doubled in number while their proportions are improved. The county offices occupy the first story. In the second are the chief court-rooms and a library almost as large as the largest court-room, which measures seventy feet by forty-five feet. In the third story are court-rooms again and a multitude of clerks' apartments, while the roof story can be put to similar use if needful. Above the third floor the five remaining stories of the tower are arranged as storage-rooms for documents, while one of its turrets holds a staircase and another an elevator, and two are ventilating shafts. Of course this is but the barest outline of a plan the minute excellence of which can only be understood by a careful com-

GRANITE CAPITAL, COURT-HOUSE, PITTSBURGH.

parison of the requirements set before the architect with his large-scale drawing.

As the work was well under way before the utilization of natural gas had purified Pittsburgh's atmosphere, Richardson gave particular care to the question of lighting, and we are told that it was his success in this direction more even than the artistic merit of his designs which determined their selection. All the main apartments are lighted from two sides, and there is not a single room in the build-

ALLEGHENY COUNTY BUILDINGS, PITTSBURGH.

JAIL, PITTSBURGH.

ing which does not receive an abundance of light through the outer walls. The heating appliances are of an elaborate kind, and the ventilating apparatus is among the most interesting features of the building. The supply of fresh air is drawn from the top of the tower through openings about two hundred and fifty feet above the ground, and after being warmed and cleansed is distributed in a volume which, it is calculated, will supply thirty cubic feet of fresh air per minute to each occupant of the Court-house. The care with which all accessory details have been considered is shown by the fact that every gas jet in the building has its special ventilating pipe.

In plan the jail is in the shape of an irregular cross the central part of which is occupied by an octagonal guard-room, forty-eight feet in diameter, which is also to be used as a chapel. One short arm of the cross contains the reception and officers' rooms, while the other arms are occupied by the tiers of cells. Two L-shaped wings at the end of the cross contain the kitchen and various service-rooms, the hospital, and the sheriff's dwelling, while the prisoners' courtyards are formed by their junction with the wings of the jail proper. The details of the plan are of the greatest interest — convenience, security, and thorough ventilation being provided for in simple yet ingenious ways.

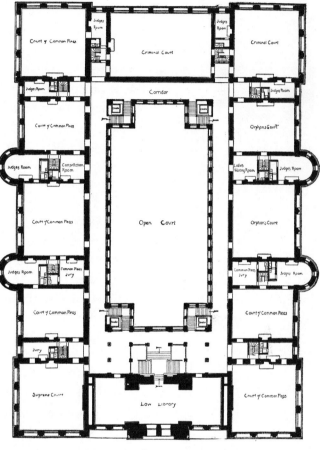

PLAN OF COURT-HOUSE (SECOND STORY), PITTSBURGH.

The treatment of the outside of the great building is shown in our illustrations. The construction throughout is fire-proof. Pinkish-gray Milford granite backed with brick is used in the street fronts, and brick for the most part in the courtyard fronts. The trimmings are of cut stone but the ashlar is rock-faced. Ornament is very sparingly used and the capitals, like the mouldings, strings, and water-tables, are kept very flat, in order to avoid the disfigurement of surface and the distortion of line which would result from the accumulation of soot upon projecting members. The building depends for its beauty upon its design properly so-called, which, while preserving a dignified symmetry between corresponding part and part, is so varied in the successive stories as to produce an effect of great grandeur combined with animation. When the plan and the perspective are studied together we find that this variation clearly expresses the varying importance and purpose of the different apartments. Above the chief entrance-porch on Grant Street (the central arch of which is thirteen feet wide by twenty feet in height) the three large arched windows light the library, while the similar ones in the third story light the supreme court room. On the other fronts the central groups of windows light the principal court-rooms, and the long arcades of the third story, which do so much to relieve the massive effect of the lower portions, open into the rows of transcribing-rooms and offices. The great gables on the side façades emphasize the place of the passage-ways which give access from the street into the court-yard. The tower is very beautiful as a piece of design and is appropriate as expressing the civic power which has its throne beneath these roofs. If it had no use but this it would still be a necessary feature from an artistic point of view; but our interest in its beauty is vastly increased when we see that various new modern needs have been met in the preservation of this traditional feature the ancient uses of which are now symbolic only. It is such a piece of work as this tower which most convincingly shows the truly creative character of Richardson's talent. The exterior of the jail is in harmony with that of the Court-house but is much more severe in treatment. The roof reveals the shape and importance of the octagonal hall, and the vast voussoirs which Richardson brought home in his mind from Spain are as appropriate in a modern prison door as in ancient portals of defense.

Taken as a whole the design of this vast and complex structure, both inside and out, is a marvel of good sense as well as of architectural beauty. None of the faults which appear in some of Richardson's other buildings can be found in this. It seems as simply yet completely right in execution as in first conception. We may take the Court-house as Richardson wished it to be taken — as the full expression of his mature power in the direction where it was most at home. Had he not lived to build it his record would still have been a surprising one and would still have entitled him to be called a man of genius in the full meaning of the term. But it would have been an incomplete, a broken record,

TOWER, COURT-HOUSE, PITTSBURGH.

while now we see the best of which he himself felt capable; and seeing it we believe that no possible problem which a long life might have brought him would have been too difficult for him to solve. It proves that he was more firmly convinced than ever that in the precedents of southern Romanesque he could find his best inspiration, but that he had worked his way to a very different attitude towards them from the one he had first assumed. The Court-house is the most magnificent and imposing of his works, yet it is the most logical and quiet. It is the most sober and severe, yet it is the most original and in one sense the most eclectic. Although all its individual features have been drawn from an early southern style, its silhouette suggests some of the late-mediæval buildings of

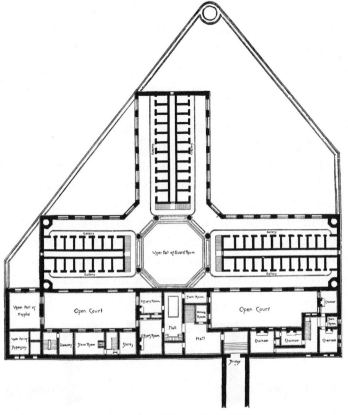

PLAN OF JAIL (SECOND STORY), PITTSBURGH.

the north of Europe, and its symmetry, its dignity and nobility of air, speak of Renaissance ideals. To combine inspirations drawn from such different sources into a novel yet organic whole while expressing a complex plan of the most modern sort — this was indeed to be original. There is no other municipal building like Richardson's Court-house. It is as new as the needs it meets, as American as the community for which it was built. Yet it might stand without loss of prestige in any city in the world.

CHAPTER XV.

THE FIELD BUILDING AND THE CINCINNATI CHAMBER OF COMMERCE.

THE Baptist Church at Newton, near Boston, which Richardson was commissioned to build in October, 1884, is interesting chiefly by reason of its plan. Pecuniary resources were limited, and the design was therefore very simple, while the ornament which will relieve its massiveness has been left in block for future execution.

Our non-episcopal congregations often ask that a church-building shall include many things besides the place of worship itself — large Sunday-school and lecture rooms, "church parlors," committee-rooms, and even kitchens to serve charitable and social needs. In providing all these at Newton Richardson adopted an expedient which worked in the interests of economy as well as of that love for architectural clearness which would have a church to look like a church and nothing else. Instead of surrounding his church with a group of minor apartments he massed these into a basement story and placed his church above them. In meeting the special needs of a Baptist congregation he designed as wisely and in a very

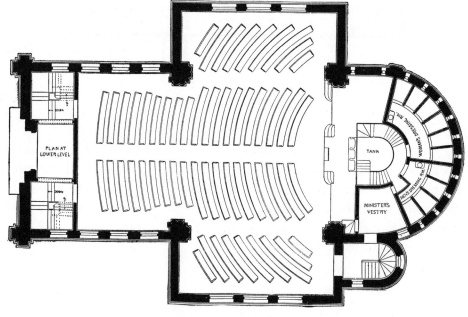

PLAN OF BAPTIST CHURCH, NEWTON.

original way. The characteristic feature of the Baptist service is the rite of immersion, but in previous churches this rite had never been architecturally recognized. The great tank or "baptistry" had not been a part of the structural design but a mere make-shift — an undignified basin sunk in the floor and boarded over when not in use ; and those who had approached or left it had been forced to pass in full sight of the congregation. Richardson's baptistry, on the other hand, is a permanent, prominent, and controlling feature in his design. The east end of his church forms a large semi-circular apse. On the chord of the apse stands the pulpit-platform and behind this is a large basin, sufficiently raised to be visible from the church and inclosed on the other three sides to a considerable height by a curtain. Beyond and above rise the circling windows of the apse, and the screened-off space between its lower walls and the curtain is filled by dressing-rooms arranged on a radiating plan. The practical good sense of the idea is not more evident than its expressional and artistic felicity.

The Field Building in Chicago stands with the Pittsburgh Court-house and the Cathedral drawings at the head of all Richardson's productions, and in spite of the unquestionable superiority, as monumental conceptions intrinsically considered, of these two works, it is in one way his most remarkable. At first sight either the Cathedral or the Court-house may seem richer in evidence of his imaginative ability. But in neither of them was his imagination compelled to begin at the very bottom of the problem. Cathedrals existed by scores, not just like the one he conceived but similar in scheme ; the type was fixed, the main features settled, the general plan prescribed ; and the minor features which he combined into a fresh result were all to be found, in suggestion at least, in the vast and varied storehouse of ancient precedents. Great municipal buildings, too, had been built for ages ; and though they imposed upon him no such ready-made outline of a scheme as did the old cathedrals, they gave at least standards of comparison by which he could anticipate the probable success of his own effort. In each case — though in each in a different way — his result is amply entitled to be called new and individual. But in neither is it based on a radically new conception.

On the other hand, a vast commercial building of the sort he was more than once bidden to design had been a thing unknown in earlier ages. The dependence of the art of architecture upon the science of construction, the dependence of this upon the practical wants of men, and the alteration of these wants by facts and inventions of seemingly slight import, were never more strikingly shown than by the genesis of the immensely tall commercial buildings of our larger towns. They were born of two distinctively American characteristics — haste and mechanical ingenuity. Our intense appreciation of the fact that time is money has made the cost of land in our large cities extraordinarily great ; for it is, of course, the wish to save time which makes us crowd our places of business so closely together. This costliness of the land inspired the wish for a greater degree of vertical extension than had previously been achieved ; and the development of the steam-lift permitted such extension to a degree limited only by constructional necessities. Architecture as an art had no voice in the new departure, but was merely bidden to make the structurally possible artistically satisfying if it could.

If general proportions were the only things prescribed to the designer, the most difficult problems of this class would be those in which lateral dimensions are narrowest. But individual features are also prescribed to him in undignified monotony. He may not boldly project and recess his masses — he would waste valuable ground. He may not conspicuously break the ridge or incline the slope of his roof — his upper story is not a garret but a space as valuable as those which lie below it. He may not group his openings and support them with broad fields of wall — his interior must be cut up into many little rooms all equally well lighted. Nor does economy or expressional truth permit him to introduce great portals, loggias, bays, or balconies. The practical ideal of a commercial building is, in short, a vast rectangular box pierced at close equal intervals with windows of moderate size. The average factory — only with exaggerated height — may stand as the type of the thing which the American architect is asked to make a work of art fit to stand in comparison in a city's finest streets with church and dwelling-house and municipal palace. It is easy to see, therefore, why the more lateral dimensions are enlarged, the greater his difficulties become ; for the larger and more self-asserting a structure, the less content we can be with a design which is simply agreeable in its individual features — the more we ask in the way of coherent dignified effect, well-balanced structural composition. And how are these qualities to be secured when, no matter what the lateral extension, height is still excessive, mass must still be unbroken, and features still petty and monotonous ?

Richardson was one of the first to try, seriously and frankly, to answer this question ; and at the time when it was built no other answer so successful as his Cheney Building in Hartford had been given. His Ames Building in Boston was an improvement even upon this — at last we had a great commercial structure which was a monument of beauty, which, far from displeasing the eye, produced a strong "architectural emotion." But the problem was not fully mastered. Beauty had been gained, but at the sacrifice of expressional truth in general effect and — a point of especial importance in a class of work which must be controlled by economical more than by purely æsthetic considerations — at the expenditure of too great an amount of money. The richly delicate ornamentation of the Ames Building is, like all good architectural decoration, so much a part and parcel of the scheme that we cannot suppress it and leave the scheme in a state to be criticised with fairness. But it means too great an outlay for the average owner to emulate ; and, even if this consideration be ignored, it means an expression which is not in accord with the purpose of the building. A store should not cost as much as a palace, and just as certainly it ought not to look like a palace.

The judgment of many other architects upon the Ames Building has expressed itself in more or less successful attempts to reproduce its general effect. Richardson himself always took great pride in its incontestable beauty ; but his true judgment of it as a type for repeated use is shown by the character of the Chicago building commissioned by Mr. Marshall Field in April, 1885. Certain structural ideas, certain main features, are common to the two ; but their treatment is widely different, and in effect and expression the earlier and the later building are utterly unlike.

The main constructional device common to the two, but far more boldly and

FIELD BUILDING, CHICAGO.

CHAMBER OF COMMERCE, CINCINNATI.

simply carried out in the Field Building, is the including of more than one story within the sweep of a range of great round-headed arches. It is not a device peculiar to Richardson but one which — partly though by no means solely as a result of his influence — is accepted by most of our able architects as the best for the purpose. It redeems the monotonous poverty of many low stories and countless little windows. It supplies features appropriate in scale to the height of the structure. It leads the eye in a horizontal direction without unduly multiplying horizontal lines. It manifests solidity; and it permits repose and animation to be combined.

The nearest approach of earlier ages to the modern problem had been made in the lofty palaces of Renaissance Italy. We know how Palladio dealt with them — diminishing their height and ennobling the relative lowness of their stories by his ranges of great pilasters. We know, too, how his bold innovation has ever since been criticised by purists. An observer of broad taste, however, may find much to say in favor of it, and still more to say in favor of our modern version of the same idea. The result which Palladio sought to produce by ornamental additions we try to produce in the process of construction; and though superficial beauty may be greater in his work, ours has a more truly architectural excellence. Our great including features form not an overlay but the fabric itself, and the included ranges of windows are integrally united with them and with one another, while their individual independence is yet clearly shown by the heavy mullions and transoms.

The Field Building is the vast rectangular box in its most uncompromising estate. The site measures three hundred and twenty-five feet by one hundred and ninety feet, and every foot of it is covered by a solid mass which rises to a height of one hundred and twenty-five feet. The roof is invisible, the doorways are inconspicuous, and decoration is very sparingly used. The whole effect depends upon the structure of the walls themselves. No building could more frankly express its purpose or be more self-denying in the use of ornament. Yet the most elaborately massed, diversified, and decorated structure could not be more truly a design; and its prime virtues of a solidity commensurate with its elevation and a dignity equal to its bulk are secured in such a way that even a high degree of beauty is not wanting. The material is fine in color — red sandstone in the upper parts and red Missouri granite in the lower. The tone of the two differs only slightly, but they are unlike, of course, in quality and are differently finished — the sandstone is cut and the granite is rock-faced. Each detail of the reticent sculptured decoration tells strongly against the general severity, and the hand of a careful, skillful artist is as plainly visible in that varied disposition of the plain units of construction which gives interest to every foot of the surface. It is visible, too, in the beautiful profile of the angles, and in that alternation of heavier with lighter piers which inconspicuously yet effectively relieves the monotony of the upper range of windows. In short, this vast, plain building is as carefully studied as the smallest and most elaborate could be, and is a text-book of instruction in treatment no less than in composition.

In August, 1885, Richardson gained in competition the commission to build for the merchants of Cincinnati their Chamber of Commerce. The work was not actually begun until after his death, but the approved design had received its final modifications under his own eye. A comparison of the illustration here given with the competition-drawing[1] will show what these modifications were — changes in the treatment of the basement, in the design of the main story on the shorter façade (making it similar to the longer), and in the pitch and elevation of the roof, all effected for the sake of greater simplicity and of more harmonious proportions. The design as it is now being carried out is most interesting in its evidence

FOUNTAIN, DETROIT.

that Richardson always in these later years felt the value of symmetry and of the repose which it secures, although he still liked to work in an ornate way when the character of the building permitted.

The problem presented by the Chamber of Commerce had not the hampering monotony of a simple commercial building, but it was quite as modern in its own way. American merchants, like their far-off predecessors in Belgium and Holland, want a great and dignified hall of assemblage; but, with a keener eye to revenue, they demand that it shall be combined with an "office building," — that every possible foot of space shall be put to use in ways that are often quite at variance with the chief use of the building, and that as many such feet as possible shall be secured by vertical extension. Richardson's problem, therefore, was, well to combine and clearly to express many apartments alien in character and discordant in idea; and it is hard to say whether its practical or its expressional difficulties were greatest.

[1] Published in the *American Architect and Building News*, September 11, 1886.

The building stands on a sloping site which measures one hundred and fifty feet by one hundred feet. The first floor and the higher portions of the basement are occupied by bank-offices, shops, and a restaurant. The second story, forty-eight feet in height, contains the great hall and its dependencies — part of it being subdivided into three tiers of small rooms. The hall is one hundred and forty feet long by sixty-eight feet wide, with a lobby forty feet by eighteen feet. The angle-pavilions form large bays in the hall itself where members may retire for private conference. The three upper stories are filled with offices, the portions above the hall being suspended from the roof by an elaborate scheme of iron construction. A knowledge of this scheme justifies, of course, the ponderousness of the roof and of the immense angle-pavilions which support it. The expressional clearness and the beauty of the exterior treatment need no fuller explanation than our illustration gives. The construction throughout is entirely fireproof. The walls are of pink Milford granite and the roof is of red tiles.

CHAPTER XVI.

RAILROAD STATIONS. — DWELLING-HOUSES.

DINING-ROOM, HOUSE OF N. L. ANDERSON, WASHINGTON.

It is much to be regretted that Richardson was never commissioned to build a great terminal railway station. His success with smaller stations proves that such a problem would have given free outlet to his talent on its strongest side.

In the year 1881 he was asked to build a small station at Auburndale, near Boston, a larger one at Palmer in the centre of the State, and another small one at North Easton. Three more were put in hand in 1883, four in the succeeding year, and two in 1885. Most of them were for rural stopping-places in the neighborhood of Boston; but one was for Holyoke, near Springfield, and another for New London, Conn., and both of these are of larger size. The last named (which was not begun until after his death) is of brick; all the others are of granite trimmed with Longmeadow stone.

A glance at any one of them shows that Richardson strove first of all clearly to express the building's purpose — to mark the fact that a station is not a house but a shelter, not a place to live in but, so to say, a place to wait under. The roof is the chief feature, not the walls. These are always low and the plan as compact as possible, while the roof is always massive and broad. In tiny wayside stations, such as that at Waban, there are no projecting sheds but the roof is carried far out on great wooden corbels. Sometimes, as at North Easton and Chestnut Hill, there is a great carriage-porch on the side away from the tracks and a long shed running beside them; and again, as at Holyoke, the shed encircles the whole building. In no two cases are the designs alike, but in all there is the same expression of temporary shelter as the main thing to be supplied, together with a sturdy air of permanence. Often this air is secured with the frankest good-sense but occasionally it results in part from features which a sternly conscientious criticism might condemn. At North Easton, for instance, three huge round-arches form the three exposed sides of the carriage-porch, supporting nothing but themselves and their own roof. They are evidently giants doing striplings' service. But they may excuse themselves, perhaps, as accenting the expressional importance of the roofs, and their beauty is so seductive — so simple yet so picturesque, so dignified yet so rural looking — that it is hard to protest against them. In fact, our country railroad stations had so long been hideous make-shifts or futile attempts at prettiness (and in either case synonyms for fragility and parsimony), that the

RAILROAD STATION, AUBURNDALE.

massiveness of Richardson's seemed a protest which would have been less welcome had it been less emphatic. Nor was it often too emphatic. The majority of his stations are as simple and right in feature as they are appropriate in general effect, while none of them show more than touch of decoration. All parts are as carefully

RAILROAD STATION, NORTH EASTON.

built and finished as in his monumental structures, all materials are dignified and durable, and all surfaces are made pleasant to the eye. The interior of the waiting-rooms is wainscoted with wood or brick, and the construction of the roof is usually shown. All necessary features are artistically treated — the fire-places (which are commonly of brick), the drinking-fountains and gas-fixtures, the settees on the exterior and the long benches within, and the ticket-offices which project upon the platform as charmingly designed bays. But no features or details exist for the sake of beauty merely, and there is no carving in stone and very little

RAILROAD STATION, NORTH EASTON.

in wood. The corbeled wooden posts which support the sheds are especially to be commended for their simplicity and their frank expression of the nature of the material.

It need hardly be added that the plan of each station was very carefully studied for convenience as well as compactness, or that each was designed with reference to its effect on its own particular site. Chestnut Hill is perhaps the prettiest example of a union of artistic and natural beauties which to some degree might always be secured in similar spots, making an hour's detention there a very different thing from that purgatory of discomfort and impatience which we are so often called upon to bear.

When an architect's leanings are distinctly toward massiveness, impressiveness, grandeur, vigor, and self-assertion, we naturally conclude that he will show less aptitude for domestic than for monumental work — especially in a land like ours

RAILROAD STATION, WOODLAND.

which asks for no palaces or castles but merely for citizens' dwellings, modest, as a rule, in all respects and even when sumptuous and costly seldom of great size. Richardson's record is in harmony with such conclusions. Indeed, it illustrates their justness even more plainly than might have been foreseen.

In his earlier years he seems to have had a comparative distaste for domestic work which amounted almost to positive dislike. He would sometimes exclaim in his over-emphatic way that " house-building is not architecture in the noble sense of the word; " and the phrase was half inspired by sincere conviction, though half, perhaps, by the feeling that house-building was not the kind of architecture in which his own success had been achieved. He was too sensible, however, and too ambitious to decline any commission which came in his way, and too true an artist not to exert himself in its fulfillment. And as commissions for houses became more frequent with the growth of his reputation, and as his results became more of an honor to that reputation, his interest increased proportionately. In the last few years of his life he felt the deepest concern and the most entire pride in the many houses he then had in hand.

The interiors of his early houses are much better than their exteriors. These are uninteresting, and in the light of to-day seem uncharacteristic, even unprophetic. Here, more evidently than in his other structures, he was working in the dark, with no clear idea of what he wished to do or of the relative value of the various schemes which presented themselves. No one of these houses represents a definite, distinct conception, while even the Agawam Bank and the Worcester

RAILROAD STATION, CHESTNUT HILL.

SKETCH FOR END OF TRINITY RECTORY.

High School do represent such conceptions, although of unsatisfactory kinds. Mr. Benjamin F. Bowles's house in Springfield, for example, was built long after these two works — in May, 1873, when Trinity Church had been in hand a year; but all there is about it which speaks of Richardson or of any strong designer is a broad plain field of brick wall at the back. The only early house which is successful as a whole is the one designed for Mr. William Watts Sherman of Newport in 1874. It is partly of stone and partly shingled, and though less simple and coherent in design than Richardson would have made it later in his life, it is picturesque, individual, and attractive. It is still among the most interesting houses in Newport.

It was not until 1879 that Richardson undertook another dwelling. Then he designed the rectory for Trinity Church in Boston. By this time his manner had become firmly established if not fully developed, and the rectory is a characteristic piece of work though by no means one to cite as really representative. The great porch and many other features are delightful; but the composition is restless and the decoration somewhat heavily out of scale. Picturesque is again the word which comes to mind, and it is not the highest word of praise for a city house.

An entrance-lodge for the country-seat of Mr. Frederick L. Ames, at North Easton, was commissioned in March, 1880. Of course it is not one of Richardson's important works, yet there is no other of any kind which has been more often illustrated, more widely discussed, or more diversely judged.

GATE LODGE, NORTH EASTON.

Its purpose is more dignified than its name implies; in addition to the lodge proper it contains a suite of bachelor apartments, and the circular end is a storage-room for plants in winter. It is built of bowlders such as were used in the Medford church, but in a more eccentric way. No stones were too big, too rough, or too abnormal in shape to claim a place in its walls, and the ashlar about the openings was made as inconspicuous as possible. Considered in themselves these walls would be brutal if they were not so amusing; but refinement is given the building by the graceful great curve of the archway (built of cut stones of many tints but all of local origin) and by the fine sweep of the simple roofs. It is too eccentric a building to be judged by the standards which we apply to Richardson's other works. Individual taste will always play a larger part than reasoned criticism in deciding upon its merits. The public has found it peculiarly attractive. Many

SKETCH OF HOUSE FOR N. L. ANDERSON, WASHINGTON.

architects have praised it in strong terms. Others have called it interesting but not beautiful. Others, again, pronounce it a mere architectural extravaganza of a semi-humorous sort, acknowledging, however, that only a vigorous mind could have been whimsical in such titanic fashion. The most serious reproach which can be brought against it is of an extrinsic character. It seems to announce the entrance to a vast park and a massive château, rather than to an American country home.

In 1881 Richardson was employed by Mr. F. L. Higginson to build a house fifty-five feet in width on Beacon Street in Boston. At the same time a New York firm of architects, two of whom (Messrs. McKim and White) had been his own pupils, were commissioned to build a house of similar size on an adjoining lot. The two designs are very different in style and spirit, but each designer, we perceive, kept a friendly eye upon the other's intentions. The same materials — Longmeadow stone and red brick — are used in both buildings, the string-courses come at the same level, the roofs are similar, and the general result is one of harmony in contrast, of artistic amity and mutual support, such as we seldom find where adjacent houses clearly confess a different parentage.

The interior of Richardson's house is very dignified, and shows the touch of a skillful planner and a master of rich yet refined decoration. But neither the reticence nor the refinement of the interior is reproduced outside. The design is bold, effective, and in parts very interesting, and the roof at least is extremely good. But as a whole this house again is too picturesque, too restless, too emphatic in decoration, and too uncompromisingly massive. And it seems less characteristic even in its defects than most of Richardson's buildings of so late a date — despite its Romanesque forms it hints at the influence of the modern English gospel of domestic architecture as preached by Mr. Norman Shaw. It shows, in short, that Richardson had not yet conceived a vital and satisfactory idea of his own with regard to the aspect which a city home should wear. When we consult our dates and find that Trinity rectory is contemporaneous with Sever Hall, and Mr. Higginson's house with the Law School and the Auburndale station, we realize how slow in every respect was his advance in domestic work.

Richardson made a great step forward, however, when he designed a red brick house for Mr. N. L. Anderson in Washington in the summer of 1881. The problem was more inspiriting than that which had offered on Beacon Street. There he had had a façade only; here he had a corner lot extensive enough to leave a large house free on every side. The house is very simple in mass, with two plainly treated bays and a lofty hipped roof. So vast is this roof that though very beautiful it strikes one more, perhaps, as an expedient to avoid the commonplace than as an obviously sensible covering for a city home in a climate where snows are light and infrequent. And the entrance also, though in an opposite way, bears the imprint of willfulness. If the roof is too self-asserting, the entrance is so very quiet that its expression is hardly in accord with its practical importance in the scheme. Yet in spite of these faults the building is a fine one — grand in mass, harmonious in proportions, coherent in design, and dignified in its severe simplicity. Here at last we have a true conception. The interior is wholly successful, well lighted, and in plan unlike our usual types of arrangement

REAR OF PERCY BROWNE'S HOUSE, MARION.

yet not at all eccentric. It has at once an aristocratic and a thoroughly comfortable air. It is a charming interior to look at and a delightful one to live in.

A country house for the Rev. Percy Browne at Marion, Mass., was designed in the last months of the same year. It is one of the smallest structures that Richardson ever built, and, I believe, the least expensive; yet in its way it is a great success. It stands on the crest of a short but steep slope overlooking a road in the outskirts of the village, beyond which lie flat meadows and the not distant sea. It is very low and comparatively very long, with many windows in broad groups, a loggia in the centre of the front, a piazza at one end and across a portion of the back, small dormers, and low but massive chimneys. Its foundations follow with delightful frankness the variations of the ground upon which it stands, while its good proportions and the harmonious arrangement of its roof-lines give it that truly architectural character in which dignity may lie for the most modest building. It is so appropriate to its surroundings that it seems to have grown out of them by some process of nature, and it is equally appropriate to its purpose. It explains itself at once as a gentleman's summer home, but with

CEILING OF HALL, HOUSE OF JOHN HAY, WASHINGTON.

a simplicity which does not put the humblest village neighbor out of countenance. Inside, the planning gives an unexpected amount of comfort and air of space. The doorways are very wide, and are so arranged as to afford a diagonal instead of a straight perspective. The windows are carefully placed to command every possible point of outlook, the rear views toward woods and sunset being as much considered as those which show the sea. The longer one studies this little house the better one likes it, the more typical it seems of that sort of excellence which the American owner so often craves — artistic treatment combined with cheapness, comfort with small dimensions, beauty with simplicity, refinement without decoration. Outside, the only touch of ornament is given by the varied shaping of the shingles, and inside, pleasant tints alone relieve the plainness of the woodwork, and good outlines the severity of the chimney-pieces. It has sometimes been said that Richardson took so much interest in great problems that he had none left to give to small ones. But no one could have more carefully studied a little house like this, the cost of which, exclusive of foundations, barely exceeded twenty-five hundred dollars.

In January, 1884, Richardson received from Mr. John Hay and Mr. Henry Adams the commission to build two adjoining houses on La Fayette Square in Washington. Mr. Hay's house stands on the corner of Sixteenth Street while Mr. Adams's has but a single façade fronting on the square. In each case certain things were prescribed of so controlling a sort that the design cannot be judged as strictly representing Richardson's own impulses. No one knew better than he, for instance, that the turret-like bay which forms the angle of the corner house tends to destroy repose, and introduces an unfortunate accent of picturesqueness into a whole which otherwise would have been of monumental dignity. Again, the singular plan of Mr. Adams's house was given in outline for his treatment. In this case, however, the demand resulted in no decrease of excellence. The chief rooms were to be upstairs, and the ground floor was to be divided longitudinally by a wall —the hall and staircase lying to the right, the kitchen apartments to the left of it, and communication between them being effected only at the back of the house. Richardson clearly marked this division on the exterior by designing his ground-story with two low, somewhat depressed arches with a pier between them. Within one arch is the beautifully treated main doorway, and behind the other, masked by a rich iron *grille*, are the windows of the servants' apartments, while the door which leads to these lies beyond the arch to the left. Inside, the hall with its great fire-place and its stairway forming broad platforms is as charming as it is individual, and the living-rooms up-stairs are well proportioned, and simple but complete in detail. The fire-places are their chief features — wide and low, with jambs and mantels of rich-toned marble which might be too heavy but for their carefully studied outlines and firm yet delicate decoration.

BRICK CARVING, HOUSE OF HENRY ADAMS, WASHINGTON.

The finest external feature of Mr. Hay's house is the doorway on Sixteenth Street — an imposing arrangement of broad steps leading up to a balustraded platform with a richly carved door set back under a powerful round arch. Inside, even the fine hall is exceeded in beauty by the dining-room, one end of which is filled by a wide mantel of green marble recessed in a deep alcove of the same material.

Both houses are built of red brick with trimmings of very light-colored Ohio stone. The plain brick surfaces as well as the carvings were carefully studied for variety in unity. The upper part of Mr. Adams's house is particularly instructive as proving what quiet yet interesting effects can be produced

STONE CARVING, HOUSE OF HENRY ADAMS, WASHINGTON.

by the diversified arrangement of plain bricks. As a whole this façade is both successful and original. The imposed conditions are partly responsible for the fact that the adjoining side of Mr. Hay's house does not combine with it quite happily; but it is inferior even as regards those details of treatment for which we

SKETCH OF HOUSE FOR J. R. LIONBERGER, ST. LOUIS.

must hold the artist altogether responsible. The main front of this house, however, including the entrance just described, is almost as good as Mr. Adams's façade and more imposing in effect. One gets a good idea of the scope of Richardson's talent by turning from the rich dignity of this house to the utter simplicity — quite as artistic in its own way — of Mr. Adams's stable.

SKETCH OF HOUSE FOR FRANKLIN MACVEAGH, CHICAGO.

In March, 1885, another large house, for Mr. B. H. Warder, was taken in hand in Washington. Although it stands in the middle of the block its plan is not determined by the usual straight façade. The width of the lot — about seventy-six feet — permitted Richardson to recess nearly one half of the front to a

HOUSE OF B. H. WARDER, WASHINGTON.

considerable distance. The space thus left free forms a carriage-entrance from which a great archway beneath the recessed wing gives access to the stables in the rear. The more prominent wing contains the great hall with the reception rooms and chief bedrooms above; the other contains the dining-room and picture-gallery and the children's apartments. The main staircase is very stately, with

SKETCH OF HOUSE FOR J. J. GLESSNER, CHICAGO.

broad platforms and carved columns that have a charming effect from a window which opens upon them from the library alcove. The dining-room and picture-gallery are connected by archways supported on delicately ornamented shafts.

The exterior is built of an almost white Ohio stone. Its design recalls a little that of the French château of Renaissance times. But the likeness is in outline

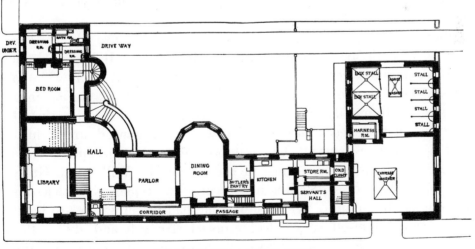

PLAN OF HOUSE FOR J. J. GLESSNER, CHICAGO.

only. The treatment is characteristic of Richardson's latest manner, to which a study of Byzantine motives gave a much greater delicacy than had marked his earlier work. As the house forms but two sides of its court-yard, and as the third is formed by the plain projecting wall of the adjoining house, there is a lack of completeness in the effect which is somewhat disturbing. But despite this fact the design has great nobility and elegance as well as individuality, and clearly expresses a beautiful and convenient interior.

During the year 1885 Richardson was commissioned to build three more large city houses — one in St. Louis and two in Chicago. They had barely been begun at the time of his death, but the illustrations represent his matured intentions and the present aspect of the buildings. The design for Mr. Glessner's house in Chicago gave Richardson peculiar satisfaction. The lot was of large size but instead of placing the house in the middle of it he placed it on the street lines and threw all the remaining space into an inclosed court-yard. Here the carriage-approach ends after passing under a great archway, and here are balconies and loggias upon which the chief apartments open. Richardson considered the scheme

SKETCH OF HOUSE FOR W. H. GRATWICK, BUFFALO.

fortunate both as affording a retirement not often secured in our city dwellings and as allowing him to build on the side street one of those plain massive walls in which he always delighted.

Richardson has been made known in England by a house which he designed just before his death for Professor Hubert Herkomer. It is possible, however, that the work does not represent him as well as we should wish. The plan had already been decided upon when he was asked to put the exterior into shape; and he was so apt to modify a design in the process of construction that it is difficult to be sure of the success of one which was not executed under his own eye or that of a trusted assistant. The last commission he accepted, two months before his death, was to build a house at Buffalo for Mr. William H. Gratwick.

As a class, Richardson's dwelling-houses are less remarkable than his public or his commercial buildings. Yet if they alone had borne witness to his talent he would have proved himself an artist of unusual strength and skill. Perhaps no one of them can be called a perfect example of success in its own direction, as we may use the words when speaking of the Quincy Library or the Pittsburgh Court-house or the Field Building or Sever Hall. But his last houses were distinctly his best, and we may believe that had he lived a few years longer he would have improved even upon these. The greatest obstacle which confronted him in this path was gradually being overcome — that impulse towards the massive, grand, and monumental which was the very gift which made him great in other paths.

CHAPTER XVII.

CHARACTERISTICS AS AN ARTIST.

SKETCH FOR A LIGHT-HOUSE.

AN artist cannot be tested as we must test almost every other man — by the average success of his results. The artist has a right to be called as great as his very greatest work. Yet the more frequently he succeeds, the higher, of course, we esteem his power. If Richardson had built nothing good but the Pittsburgh Court-house he would still be entitled to the name of a great architect; but it is only when we consider all his works together, as in a chronological panorama, that we realize the strength of his endowment. We cannot help judging them by a stricter standard than we apply to the works of others, yet even so we are astonished to find how few of them fall below a level of great excellence.

The fact seems the more remarkable when we note the versatility they reveal. This quality has sometimes been denied to Richardson; but only by those to whom versatility means a constant change in the garments of thought, not a constant freshness in thought itself. After his art matured he adhered to a single style. But to deny his versatility for this reason is as unjust as it would be to deny a poet's because he had expressed ideas of wide diversity in a dramatic or a lyric or an epic form alone. When, moreover, we analyze the similarity in style which marks Richardson's maturer works, we find that it cannot be called uniformity. It reduces itself to terms of very broad significance. Neither in deciding upon general outlines and proportions, nor in choosing special features, nor in elaborating details, did he work after set schemes or narrow rules. A man who could immediately follow up so romantic a structure as Trinity Church with so sedate a one as Sever Hall, and who could design in the same year the picturesquely varied Chamber of Commerce and the grandly monotonous Field Building, cannot be accused of mannerism. The more we study Richardson's works the more we feel that something deeper than style constitutes their individuality — that we must look behind his round arches and square - sectioned openings, his stone mullions, his arcades and loggias, and his Byzantinesque decoration to find the fundamental qualities which really reveal him.

These qualities are: Strength in conception; clearness in expression; breadth in treatment; imagination; and a love for repose and massive dignity of aspect, and often for an effect which in the widest meaning of the word we may call "romantic." The first is the most fundamental and important quality, and upon it depends to a very large degree the presence of the others.

The chief thing which made Richardson's works alike among themselves and unlike the works of almost all his contemporaries was his power to conceive a building as a whole, and to preserve the integrity of his conception no matter how various might be the features or how profuse the decoration he employed. Each of his best buildings is an organism, an entity, a coherent vital whole. Reduce it by distance to a mere silhouette against the sky, or draw it down to a thumb-nail sketch, and it will still be the same, still be itself; yet the nearer we approach it the more its individuality will be emphasized. This is because its character depends upon no one feature, no one line, but upon the concord of all and the vigor of the impression which all together give. No feature is of dominant importance, but each is of the right relative importance from any given point of view, and all are vitally fused together; — the building seems to have grown, developed, expanded like a plant. We cannot dismember it in thought without hurting both what we leave and what we take away; and whether we study it up or down — from particulars to generals or from generals to particulars — there is no point where conception seems to end and mere treatment to begin. It would be as impossible, without injuring the conception, to change the surface character of the walls or the distribution of the ornament, as to alter the relative proportions of walls and roof or the size and position of the chief constructional features. When these facts are perceived together with the great difference in general aim which exists between Richardson's best buildings, his versatility is by implication confessed. It matters nothing that he drew from the same historic source most of the elements with which he built church and warehouse, civic palace and country cottage. In each case a radically different idea was needed and in each case it came to him.

In each case, too, it came as a strikingly appropriate idea. While conceiving and developing a structure as a whole, he worked from the inside out, not from the outside in. The nature of the service it should render was his first thought, its plan his next; and these rule his exterior in its major and its minor features. We do not find him taking schemes or features which were beautiful because appropriate in one building and trying to make them beautiful in another at the expense of fitness; and there is no favorite feature he does not sacrifice if fitness demands — not the last trace of decoration, not the visible roof which he loved to make so prominent, nor the round arch itself. Of course he sometimes sinned against perfect appropriateness of expression, but his slips were few, and the longer he lived the rarer they became. Here lies the true greatness of Richardson's works — in the fact that they are true conceptions, clearly expressing an idea as appropriate as vigorous. The great value of the Quincy Library, for instance, or of the Pittsburgh Court-house, or — at the other end of the scale — of the Marion cottage, lies in the fact that it is a coherent vital entity and at the same time a speaking entity — unmistakably a library, a municipal palace, a gentleman's seaside home.

Another fundamental quality in Richardson's work is breadth of treatment. It is this which gives his results their air of "bigness" — not the actual size which in many of them chances to be great. Artistically speaking, his smallest structures are as big as his largest, and they are so because they are as largely treated. Whatever his faults he never worked in a small, hesitating, feeble way. Clearness in aim and strength in rendering were the gods of his idolatry in art. If combined with refinement, so much the better; if not, they were still to be preferred to refinement without them. We are sure that he excused the faults of a Rubens on canvas, of a Michael Angelo in architecture, but never those of a painter who had microscopically elaborated a weak conception, of an architect who had delicately adorned a fabric that was not in the true sense a building. In his own work he was over-exuberant at times, but, so to say, with a broad brush and a vigorous touch, and with that truly architectural instinct which makes ornament accentuate the meaning of constructional lines. Of course it was the strength of his basic conception which encouraged him to be thus broad and definite in treatment. There was no temptation to fritter away his effect when he felt that his fundamental idea would impress the imagination and charm the eye. There was every reason why he should present this idea as frankly as possible, either in bold simplicity or with lavish decoration which emphasized leading lines and important features. I have said that the greatness of his work rests first of all upon the strength and the appropriateness of his conceptions; but perhaps the breadth of treatment through which they were expressed is as important a quality. Certainly it is as rare a quality in modern art.

The strong imaginative power which Richardson's works reveal should perhaps not be called a separate characteristic, being implied in the existence of those just named. Yet we realize it most fully when we understand not only how strong and vital his conceptions are and how unlike each other, but how unlike they most often are to the conceptions of any earlier day or of modern men in any other land. He took the elements of the language with which he voiced his thoughts from other thinkers, but his thoughts were his own. Whenever fitness demanded — and with our novel needs this was very often the case — he took counsel of his own imagination, began at the bottom of the problem, and produced a result which differed essentially from all others. Yet he was too true an artist to prize novelties as such, and he had too strong a faith in the individuality of his talent to fear that if he were not "original" he would not seem himself. He never needlessly sought for a new conception. It could never have occurred to him to wish merely to do something unlike what his predecessors had done or what he himself had already done. When a problem presented itself which was similar to some preceding problem, he frankly re-adapted the same idea which had already served. His versatility developed in the only way that it could have developed hand-in-hand with excellence — through the effort to fulfill the given task in the best possible manner, to find clear and full expression for the appropriate idea.

When such qualities as these are found conspicuous and persistent in an artist's work, his choice of style seems a matter of secondary importance. His thoughts have made his work great and individual, not the language in which he has expressed them. Yet Richardson's choice of language was by no means fortuitous or without deep and interesting significance. It is true that working in some other style he might as clearly have shown us the value of definiteness in conception and breadth in treatment, of harmonious effects of color and strong effects of light and shade; the beauty of a roof, the meaning of a wall; the nature of good surface treatment and of decoration which explains construction. But his chosen style was essentially favorable to the teaching of such lessons, as well as to the display of that romantic kind of beauty for which he had so strong a liking. And better than any other style it could meet his fundamental love for massiveness and repose.[1]

When he recognized the serviceableness of its forms he instinctively preferred to study them in their southern developments. His temperament was essentially a southern one — loving breadth and light and color, variety and luxuriance, not cold grandeur, solemnity, and mystery. Refinement was not one of his most fundamental qualities as an artist. Yet his steady development towards a refined simplicity could not have had its starting-point in a paraphrase of Norman work. It could only have begun with such a paraphrase of southern Romanesque as we see in the Woburn Library.

In matters of treatment Richardson's attitude towards the precedents of ancient art was the same as in matters of conception. He studied them with love and care but in no slavish, idolatrous mood, and from a practical or purely æsthetic, not from an antiquarian standpoint. He viewed them as the work of men of like nature with himself, not of demi-gods inspired to a quality of performance which modern men need not try to improve upon. They were helps for him not fetishes, starting-points not patterns. What he wanted was their aid in building a good structure, not their prescriptions how to build a " scholarly " one. He looked upon them as a dictionary not as a grammar, and still less as a collection of attractive features which might be stowed away in the mind like quotations isolated from their context. None of his pupils ever heard him say, " This is a charming thing — some day we must manage to use it." The context, he knew, was what made the worth of an architectural phrase. Only when a man is sure of

---

[1] By repose is not here implied quietness in the sense of simplicity of surface and a moderate number of features, but structural repose — repose of line and mass, repose in the form of features; and it is not too much to say that Richardson could best secure this quality by developing the suggestions of Romanesque art. Greek art, making all its lines straight and its horizontal accentuations preponderant, does not express repose so much as great strength gracefully bearing a downward pressing load. We realize the fact when we study Egyptian art, which is similar in essence to Greek, minus the grace. Gothic art, accenting vertical lines, actually expresses motion — an upward lifting as of a growing tree; so much so that when, as in its Venetian forms, it strives to be more restful, we feel that it is not really itself, that it is trying to achieve a result which could have been more perfectly secured with round arches. Roman art, when it passed from the engineer's into the artist's hand, was not a simple concrete scheme, but a splendid bastard mingling of two alien schemes. Only when it was again stripped of its Greek overlay did it clearly reveal its intrinsic qualities. It is in Romanesque art only, and in those early Renaissance modes which were directly based upon it, that we find that balance between vertical and horizontal accentuations which means perfect repose. The semicircle demands neither that ascending lines nor that retreating lines shall preponderate; and in itself it is neither passive like the lintel nor soaring like the pointed arch. It seems to have grown to its due bearing power and thus to remain, vital yet restful, making no effort either to resist downward pressure or to press upward itself.

the general meaning he wants to express, the general effect he wants to produce, can he turn to his predecessors for assistance.

In minor as in major matters Richardson invented when he was obliged to and borrowed when he could. He took the Romanesque art of the south of France as his chief but not as his only quarry. He was ready to draw from other sources any special features which a special need required; — later mediæval fashions furnished him with much material at the outset of his life, and towards its end he was more and more attracted by Byzantine forms and decorations. Whatever he took he remodeled as freely as he saw fit, and there was no more effort to conceal his alterings than his borrowings. What he wished was simply that to an intelligent eye his work should look right in the outcome; and if it did, then he knew it was right, though to a dull eye it might seem a copy or though to an antiquarian eye all the precedents of all the ages might seem to protest against it. Sometimes, of course, he was not entirely successful in his adaptations. But often he was, as in that tower of Trinity, the genesis of which has been described at length because it so clearly typifies his constant way of working. No one could mistake this tower for an ancient one, wherever it might chance to stand. Yet the impression it produces is similar to that which good ancient works produce — an impression as of a vital, homogeneous entity. And, it cannot be too often said, this is the impression made by all of Richardson's best structures. Therefore, the more eclecticism appears when they are analyzed, the more cheering is their evidence with regard to the future of our art. In nothing did Richardson do us better service than in proving that the modern artist need not be cowed into a purist, straightened into an archæologist, cramped and confined within the limits of a single narrow stretch of by-gone years — or, on the other hand, thrown wholly on his own inventive powers — if he would do work to satisfy and delight us as the men of early years satisfied and delighted themselves. The tendencies of American art have been chiefly towards a reckless inventiveness. Those of foreign art are too strongly towards mere scholasticism. But Richardson, keeping to a middle path, worked as those whom we call the demi-gods had worked. Eclecticism is more patent in his results than in theirs, for the store of precedents which lay open to him was vastly wider than that upon which any of them could draw. But in spirit his process was the same as theirs. Many other modern artists have shared this spirit theoretically but very few have had the power to express it in work which can be compared with his for excellence. Few, indeed, have had the boldness to attempt the task as frankly. It is hard to say which fact proves Richardson's independence of mind and self-trust more — the fact that he dared so visibly to borrow the general scheme of so famous a piece of work as the Salamanca tower, or the fact that having borrowed it he dared to remould it with so radical a hand. One success of this kind is a better lesson for after-comers than a hundred correct and scholarly plagiarisms. Nor need we ask the antiquary whether or no it is a success. Perhaps he might say that the builders of Salamanca would not have approved of the tower of Trinity. But very likely the builders of the Parthenon or even of the Pantheon would not have approved of Salamanca. The world has had too much — infinitely too much — of such appeals to the artistic conscience of the past. It is time to remember that the past itself never had any artistic conscience except that of the current age, and that we in our turn should make the present our judge — or that if we look outside the present it should be forward and not back. The true question to be asked with regard to work like Richardson's is whether it has those fundamental qualities of harmony, vitality, appropriateness, meaning, and beauty which will make it seem good in the eyes of men born seven hundred years from now. How it would have looked in the eyes of men born seven hundred years ago — incapable of understanding our conditions, of sympathizing with our tastes, of seeing the currents which have been all this time at work in science and in art — is indeed a matter of small concern.

Yet, as has been hinted, there is another danger besides that which lies in an overweening respect for the past. We Americans are more ready than the rest of the world to acknowledge that adaptation, not imitation, should be the artist's formula. But we do not realize all that is meant by our own words when we add that of course adaptation must be sensible and skillful. We do not realize that it needs not only more power but more knowledge and labor to adapt well than to copy well. Here again Richardson's example is infinitely instructive. He adapted well — so well that the process was a creative one in the truest sense of the word — because he had thoroughly studied the principles of his art, and because he practiced it with an exceptional degree of love and patience.

CHAPTER XVIII.

CHARACTERISTICS AS AN ARTIST.

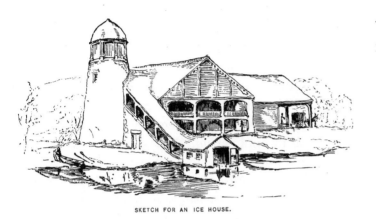

SKETCH FOR AN ICE HOUSE.

WITH regard to the benefit which Richardson received from his long early training, I cannot do better than quote the words of a brother architect :[1] —

" Richardson stands as a beacon light before the community, not only as a producer of distinguished architecture, but as a warning to impatient aspirants and their guardians against loose fancies on the subject of the education of the architect. He was no exemplar of the popular notion that all that creative genius has to do is to stretch forth its hand, however untrained, to accomplish everything that its heaven-born instinct impels it to. *Poeta nascitur, non fit,* it is true, but once born he cannot voice himself without mastering the symbols and signs of expression, and the more completely he masters them the more thoroughly and recognizably he will project himself. When once Richardson had passed through the chrysalis stage, he could not help designing in a grand way because he was a man of large calibre, of broad scope, and of lavish temperament. But he served a long apprenticeship, quite beyond the twelve or twenty-four months assigned by the average American parent as the unproductive pupillary stage of the gifted offspring. . . . The Ecole course tends chiefly . . . to classic Renaissance expression, but that counted for little. The main thing is to get the discipline. The teacher's bias is nearly immaterial. Richardson's bent led him before long to handle the grammar of a certain architectural school closer than any other, though he almost always allowed himself entire freedom in the handling. But if by any chance his instincts or moods had led him to take hold of some other vehicle of expression than the one which soon became his choice, his training, we may be sure, would have stood him in equally good stead, and he would have equally mastered and equally illustrated it."

It is more difficult to explain the patient enthusiasm of Richardson's labor to those who never had the chance to follow — either at the time or afterwards in drawings and descriptions — the genesis of one of his great structures. When a new problem appealed to him, some definite idea of a solution was very quickly

[1] A. J. Bloor, in *The Building Budget,* July, 1886.

born. But he was not quick to call it a good idea except in so far as it might seem rich in possibilities of improvement. Speaking of some fresh scheme he often said, " It is good, is n't it ? But I mean to make it better. I don't see how just yet, but I shall find out." Meanwhile he seemed less to think about it than to wait for suggestions to present themselves. " I wait," he would say, " and go to bed on it, and carry it about with me while I am doing other things, and don't try to worry it out ; and then after a while it comes." The artist as opposed to the manufacturer of art speaks in words like these ; but it is only the well-trained artist who can be thus semi-passive to good purpose, and who, when the inspiration has come, will realize that it is but the beginning of the matter. Richardson never forgot that only time and effort can turn a " good idea " into a good piece of work. It has been shown — though only in part — how he labored over Trinity Church, and how different its present aspect is from his first designs. So he always labored — not too proud to see when he had started wrong or too indolent to begin afresh, never satisfied with a thing which others found good if he could better it, never feeling himself beyond the necessity for a perpetual self-criticism broad in reach and minute in application, always open to fresh inspirations, always ready to take intelligent hints from his subordinates, always eager and ardent yet always trying to check impulse by reason. As his intelligence developed and his experience increased, his processes grew quicker and, naturally, left behind them less conspicuous traces than have been preserved in the case of Trinity. But they were always the same processes and always brought increase of excellence, as may be seen by comparing the competitive designs for the Pittsburgh Court-house with the finished building.

" About a fortnight before Richardson's death," writes Mr. Frederick Law Olmsted, " I was with him in Washington, and it is remarkable that he was led to speak in this last interview that I had with him of a point of professional economy of which he had been led to speak (by seeing a lot of rough tracings on a drawing-board) the first time he came to my house fifteen years before.

" When I came into his room in Washington he was in a reclining-chair, so exhausted after an attempt to take the air in a carriage that he had been for some time, as he explained, on the verge of losing consciousness. His eyes were blood-shot, his face red, his forehead studded with beads of sweat. He spoke feebly, hesitatingly, and with a scarcely intelligible husky utterance. While in this condition — I had been urging him and he had promised to go home the next day — a client came in. Something was said of the drawings of the structure Richardson was building for him, and then of the many successive drawings that had been made, revising the preliminary studies, the design always gaining as a turn of one detail led to the reconsideration of another, the gain being, as was intimated, steadily in the direction of simplification. Going on from this, Richardson repeated what he had first said to me at Staten Island. This was, in effect, that the most beguiling and dangerous of all an architect's appliances was the T-square, and the most valuable were tracing-paper and india-rubber. Nothing like tracing over tracing, a hundred times. There was no virtue in an architect more to be cultivated and cherished than a willing spirit to waste drawings. Never, never, till the thing was in stone beyond recovery, should the slightest indisposition be indulged to review, reconsider, and revise every particle of his work, to throw away his most enjoyed drawing the moment he felt it in him to better its design.

"From something like this he went on discussing for the better part of an hour, growing to sit up erect, his voice becoming clear, his utterance emphatic, his eyes flashing, smiling, laughing like a boy, really hilarious, much as in some of our all-night debates years ago in Albany when he was yet a lithe, active, healthy fellow. I was afraid it would be too much for him, and, rising to go, said, 'Eidlitz asked me to let him know how I found you: I shall have to tell him, never better in your life;' and he laughingly assented."

One phrase of Richardson's, repeated here, hints at something which it is important to make plain. An architect's revisings, he believed, should never end until his building is "in stone, beyond recovery;" and he exemplified this belief by altering much and often after construction had been actually begun. No one could have used preparatory pencil and paper more conscientiously, yet it was one of his firmest dogmas that they could not be implicitly trusted. If his scorn was great for the recklessness which says, No matter about the drawings — we can set things right as we build, it would have been just as great for the closet-spirit which should say, No matter how the work is looking as it grows — it was all right on paper. "The architect," he often explained, "acts on his building, but his building reacts on him — helps to build itself. His work is plastic work, and, like the sculptor's, cannot be finished in a drawing. It cannot be fully judged except in concrete shape and color, amid actual lights and shadows and its own particular surroundings; and if when it is begun it fails to look as it should, it is not only the architect's privilege but his duty to alter it in any way he can." Therefore he kept his judgment awake until his last stone was set and his last touch of decoration had been given. Therefore, too, he thought needful those long frequent hurried journeys which must have done so much to sap his strength. His representatives on the ground were capable and conscientious. He knew that he could trust them to carry out a design quite faithfully. But he could trust only his own eye to see whether the design was carrying itself out well or not, and so would leave the sick-room to find how some far-off building looked which he had seen but a few weeks before. As long as he possibly could he kept up his custom of making monthly tours through all the distant towns where he had work under way; and when journeys were at last forbidden he sent one of his chief assistants to bring him back verbal reports, and exacted daily detailed letters by means of which he could follow the placing of every stone.

There are many architects, I believe, who hold a different creed from the one which Richardson exemplified. They point with pride to the exact correspondence between their studies and their completed buildings while Richardson delighted to explain the disparities in his. It would be idle to try to lay down rules of right and wrong as decisive between such opposite ways of thinking; yet the paramount success of Richardson's results should at least be taken into account by those whose own theories and methods are not yet established.

The chief faults which have been charged against Richardson as an artist are: Extravagance; a willingness to secure a striking effect at the cost of conscientious care for all parts of a building; a neglect for the expression of construction; and a lack of refinement.

In one sense Richardson was certainly extravagant — or, to speak more exactly, lavish. He always wished to spend enough money on a building to make it perfect, and his ideas of perfection were high. In consequence, he often persuaded his clients into a larger outlay than they had anticipated. But if thus to persuade clients is not exactly a virtue it is at least a common sin — a sin into which almost every artist falls who has any skill in argument. And Richardson was not extravagant in the sense of wasting the money he secured. Few of his clients will deny that, whether or no they were right in spending so much money, they received a full return in greater beauty for the greater outlay.

His ideas of perfection, I repeat, were high. They often included the richest decoration and always that solidity which means costly methods of construction. His railroad stations cost a great deal more than had ever before been paid for stations of their size; his commercial structures were built throughout of stone; and his Capitol apartments are sumptuous to an unprecedented degree. But in neither case did he waste money in realizing an aim which might have been more cheaply realized, and in neither was the aim inappropriate to the purpose of the building. It is true that his stations might have been cheaper and still have been good; but it is not true that if they had been cheaper they would have been as beautiful, still less that they ought to have been cheaper in order to be excellent. The case is just the same with his commercial work if we take the Field Building as representative of his full development; and even the Capitol apartments are not too sumptuous for the fitting accommodation of the representatives of a commonwealth so rich and powerful as New York. They might have been less costly but there is no intrinsic, artistic reason why they should have been.

It should also be said that cases were not rare in which Richardson paid the closest regard to questions of economy. The very low cost of his successful little house at Marion has been referred to, and his other country houses were also cheap considering their excellence. The Baptist Church at Newton was given to him to build after several other architects had decided that no good church could be built for the stipulated sum; and he built it throughout of stone. Even the Field Building would have been much less costly had he carried out the first intention, which he thoroughly approved, and constructed it of brick. It was in answer to his client's wish that he substituted stone and recast the drawings he had already prepared.[1] He did not often insist upon the costlier material as an absolute necessity; but when the character of the building permitted he was always eager to use it, and he always did insist upon some kind of material and of treatment which should be commensurate in dignity with the given place and purpose.

We have very good reason, therefore, to rejoice that Richardson often secured the chance to make his buildings as sumptuous as appropriateness allowed. Our public needed to be taught two complementary truths — that architectural excellence need not always be costly, and that some kinds of architectural excellence cannot be cheap. It needed a sight of beautiful simplicity to convince it that

---

[1] As it stands the Field Building cost $800,000. The Chamber of Commerce will cost about $500,000.

neither nakedness nor cheap elaboration should ever be allowed; but it also needed a sight of really rich monumental beauty to convince it that niggardly attempts at grandeur are absurd.

The charge that Richardson was apt to neglect some parts of his buildings in order to secure the effectiveness of other parts seems merely to mean a belief that his exteriors are more complete and beautiful than his interiors. No belief could be more mistaken; — as a rule they are quite as carefully conceived and quite as carefully completed. They show the same harmony between part and part and the same uniting of all parts to produce a single impression. In this respect their influence has been very good, especially as regards those private interiors where we are apt to think that interest must mean variety, and that the character of different apartments cannot be explained without a change of style. Richardson always made his interiors consistent in style, and, whenever he had his own way, he made them as beautiful as consistency to the exteriors prescribed. That this fact is too commonly disputed is due in part to ignorance — an exterior is much more often seen than an interior and much more often portrayed; but it is also due in part to the perennial temptation which besets a critic to dwell more upon occasional failures than upon frequent virtues. Some of Richardson's interiors are certainly bare and poor in effect as compared with the outside of the buildings, and a great deal has been said about the most conspicuous case in point — the Albany City Hall. Richardson explained this case by saying that as the money at command was not sufficient to make the whole building what it should have been, he preferred to perfect the exterior at the expense of the interior rather than let both suffer together; and he would have held a similar explanation good in any other case, although I think that with a dwelling-house he would have chosen the interior as entitled to his preference. Whether it is a justifiable explanation or not — whether it argues a right adherence to his artistic ideals or an excessive wish to show himself at his best — is a question that the reader can decide for himself. But it includes the whole question as to Richardson's artistic conscientiousness. No one can think that he willingly neglected or degraded any part of any piece of work, or that he was unable to see when any part failed to equal the rest. There are mistakes in his buildings, of course, and they are sometimes of a sort which seems to sacrifice a practical to an artistic requirement — as when we find that one or two of his libraries and stations are not quite well enough lighted, and remember his love for broad, plain fields of wall and for heavy mullions and transoms. But I do not think there is any proof that he ever made such mistakes of deliberate intention; and they did not occur in his latest years.

In how far Richardson sinned against architectural ethics by concealing or misrepresenting his constructional expedients is too technical a question to be examined here. It may be said, however, that the charge seems to rest solely upon his treatment of the interior of Trinity Church. It is certainly needless to add that such sins as the misrepresentation of a plan by an exterior, or the mendacious imitation of one material in another, cannot be laid to his account. Judged by modern standards he seems singularly conscientious in such matters.

The final charge — that Richardson's work lacks refinement — is true as regards many of his earlier productions. But had the reverse been true he would have been either a weaker artist or a miracle among men. If he had cared for refinement more than for clearness and force, it would have been a proof of that innate feebleness out of which nothing strong can ever grow; and if, in breaking a new path, in formulating a new architectural language, he had been able to secure all excellences together and make executive skill go hand-in-hand with creative power from the very outset, we should be forced to credit him with an almost superhuman gift. His progress was as steadily from crudeness and rough vigor to refinement as it was from over-elaboration to simplicity. The growing refinement of his feeling for general forms shows in his growing love for serenity and symmetry. The "romantic" side of his nature still spoke in such a work as the Chamber of Commerce, but far more reticently than in those earlier efforts which have been called "barbaric," and there is no trace or hint of it in the almost classic severity and repose of the Pittsburgh Court-house. The same progress is as apparent in individual features — no later work shows such exaggerated features as the dwarf yet titanic columns of the North Easton Town Hall — and in decorative details. At the outset his decoration had been too emphatic in scale and too loose in execution, while his "barbaric" impulses had found expression in Gothicizing monsters and conspicuous gargoyles. But a more modern, which also means a more classic, spirit gradually possessed him. The delicate influence of Byzantine decoration was gradually absorbed, and no architect of our time has done work which is more pure and lovely than Richardson's wood-carvings at Quincy, more graceful yet spirited than his sculptures in the senate chamber, more simple and elegant than the fittings in some of his houses, more quiet and dignified than the plain capitals which his use of granite made appropriate at Pittsburgh. If there is a fault in the Field Building it came from his wish to avoid any over-emphatic accent; — the cornice might perhaps have been bolder in section and in motive. In fact, when we look at Richardson's best decoration we wonder how so much delicacy of thought and touch could have been evolved from the same mind which showed such strength in matters of general treatment; and when we look at any one of his latest buildings, we wonder how in that short life his exuberant spirit could have learned so large a measure of self-restraint, serenity, and good taste.

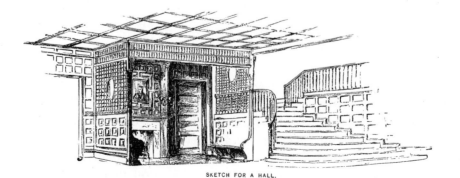

SKETCH FOR A HALL.

LIBRARY OF H. H. RICHARDSON.

CHAPTER XIX.

METHODS OF TEACHING.

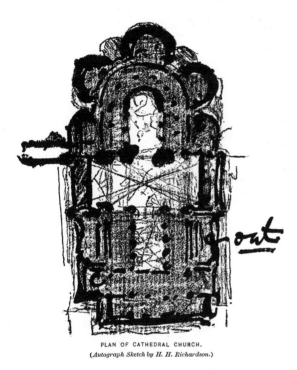

PLAN OF CATHEDRAL CHURCH.
(*Autograph Sketch by H. H. Richardson.*)

AFTER dissolving his partnership with Mr. Gambrill, Richardson never thought of forming another. It is impossible to imagine him in mature life as willing to work upon equal terms with any one else. He found it hard enough to bear the checks and limitations which came to him from his clients, and could not have consented to a division of authority in his office or have held himself accountable to any one in matters of art or business; he was too much the born autocrat and his individual ideas and personal fame had grown too dear to him. Yet he had especial need of such help as most architects get from their partners, and he received it from the devoted service of a large band of scholars the ablest of whom he quickly developed into competent assistants.

The burden of initiative impulse, constant criticism, and final oversight which he kept for his own shoulders implied extraordinary vigor and flexibility of mind. But the share of executive work and temporary responsibility which it was impossible for him to retain could only have been borne by men who had been trained in his own ideas, and in whose knowledge, judgment, and sympathy he could confide. In this pushing, eager land the temptation to a precocious assertion of independence is so strong that it was surprising and delightful to find an office like Richardson's — composed of an unusual number of students, working in an unusually independent way, yet to a singular degree a unit in feeling, effort, and production. It was no great government *atelier* supported and controlled by official prestige and direction. The smallest provincial office was not more unallied and private. Yet it was filled with a score of workers ranging in age and grade from the boyish novice up to the capable, experienced artist, all fraternally bound together and loyally devoted to their chief, all laboring together on work which had a single inspiration and a common accent, and each feeling a personal pride in results which the world knew as the master's only. Two or three of Richardson's pupils remained with him for exceptionally long periods, but in general their term of service was not more than six or seven years. It was the character of their service, the spirit in which it was rendered, and the master's method of controlling it, which made this office so different from others.

Richardson was a born teacher as well as leader, and was the most interesting and sympathetic of masters. Young men rarely speak of a former "chief" as his speak of him — with so much professional admiration joined to so much personal

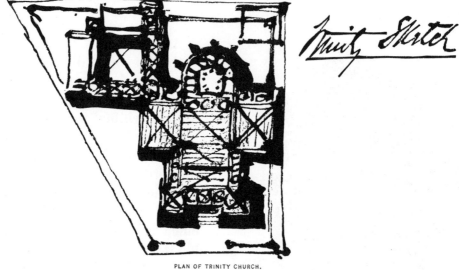

PLAN OF TRINITY CHURCH.
(*Autograph Sketch by H. H. Richardson.*)

gratitude and affection. They know and delight to confess that much as they did for him he did more for them, and was their warm friend as well as their capable, devoted instructor. The personal bond between them would under any conditions have been strong, but was drawn closer still by the way in which Richardson's home and office were connected.

The house in Brookline to which he removed while Trinity was being built was a simple, old-fashioned dwelling, with an acre or two of well-shaded ground about it. On the left of the entrance were the parlor and dining-room with a library beyond, and on the right was an unused chamber. This last was appropriated to working purposes, and was Richardson's only office for some time after he had given up the one in New York. When more room was needed the library was taken, the students having to pass from one apartment to the other through the family living-rooms. Then the room first used was abandoned, and an office for his men was built out beyond the library, which became Richardson's private study; and as the staff increased from year to year the general office was extended in an irregular line trending back parallel to the kitchen wing of the house. The additions thus made were of the simplest character, mere low working-cells which opened on one side into a long passage-way. But a few years before his death Richardson added to them at the farther end a large and sumptuous library of semi-fireproof construction; and the irregular space thus inclosed by the walls of house and office and library was eventually roofed in and lighted from above, making a great work-room on the wide walls of which the largest drawings could be displayed.

It was a curious and most interesting experience to pass from the house into the long passage-way with the " coops," as the students called them, on one hand and the big work-room on the other, all filled with busy draughtsmen, and then suddenly to come into the beautiful library which was so expressive of the master's tastes and occupations. It is a large, low-ceiled room from which by a wide arch-way opens a smaller study. The vast recessed fire-place with its old Venetian *landier* of wrought-iron, the low book-cases filled with costly architectural works and hundreds of carefully-arranged photographs, the table twelve feet square piled with objects of beauty and of use, the huge comfortable window-seats and chairs and sofas, and the walls lined with photographs and drawings, were entirely appro-priate to the needs and likings of a man who loved beauty and work in equal measure, and who liked quite as well to have space and comfort and " everything big " about him. Even at first sight Richardson's library had not the aspect of those rooms filled to overflowing with miscellaneous bric-à-brac which in recent years we have come to know so well. It was just as full and its contents were just as varied, but the general effect was harmonious and restful; there was no rub-bish among the things which professed to be works of art, there were no ugly objects of utility, and each item bore witness to the strong personal tastes and the actual material or professional needs of the owner. It was evidently in the first place a room to work in, although it was so charming a room to lounge in that even the casual visitor was loath to leave it. Its contents were the tools of its owner, and its charm was the natural outcome of the fact that his work was art. Superfi-cially the library was in striking contrast to the offices through which one entered it, but essentially there was no contrast. The one was simply the result and

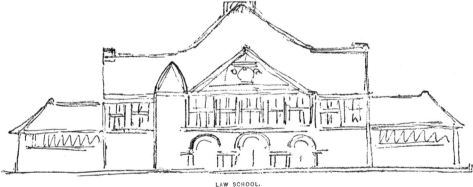

LAW SCHOOL.
(Autograph Sketch by H. H. Richardson.)

complement of the others, a splendid flower into which their utilitarianism had appropriately bloomed. And the whole place — house, offices, and library together — was so characteristic of Richardson that one can hardly think of it to-day as occupied by any one else, or find in it half the interest and charm which were so singularly potent while he lived. It expressed his energy and his success as clearly as his peculiar needs and fancies, while the unusual juxtaposition of home and work-shop kept one always in mind of the precarious state of health which had prescribed it, and therefore of the difficulties amid which energy had persisted and success had been achieved.

Though the union between house and office was more intimate at the beginning than afterwards, they were never really divided. The life of the home and the life of the office went on together. The rich library was as free to others as to Richardson himself. His photographs were pinned about to decorate the " coops," — he said he liked " to guess at what was in a boy " by the choice he made among them. The elder students were constantly at his hearth and table

PLAN OF CITY HALL, ALBANY.
(*Autograph Sketch by H. H. Richardson.*)

and seemed as much a part of his family as the children whom he loved to have about him while at work and to take with him on his hurried business journeys. So close, in fact, was the union of domestic life and professional activity, so large and yet so corporate the troop of pupils, so devoted to their chief, so conscious of their dependence upon him and of his upon them, and of the profit and honor the connection brought them, that a visit to Brookline seemed to carry one leagues and ages away from the America of the moment. One could think of nothing but some great home-studio of those elder times when leadership and coöperation in art were the rule and not the exception, when the artist lived in his work and with his scholars, and when the names of " master " and " pupil " had something of a paternal and a filial sound.

Richardson profited much by such an order of things but his students profited not less. It gave them a sense of rooted existence, of mutual dependence, of intimate comradeship, of responsibility to collective interests, which both fostered and purified their ambition, and which cultivated them in a much broader way than professional education usually does, developing them as men and not only as artists. No tendencies in modern life are more deplorable than those which lead us to disassociate our working from our living, which tempt us to think we can work well enough when we have studied just a little, and which persuade us that to do one kind of work we need only one kind of education. Against all these tendencies the spirit of Richardson's office protested, and the good influence of its protest has been felt far outside the ranks of the men who labored there.

His own personal ways of thinking and working assisted this happy influence. No young man could fail to respect his art or could approach it merely as a business in sight of a devotion so fervid, an ambition so far-reaching yet so conscientious in all that concerned the claims of art as art. None could think lightly of his share in the common task when its importance was so vigorously impressed upon him. None could be listless with such energy to reproach him, — it seemed easy to work even into the small hours of the night with a master who worked too in spite of pain and illness, cared for the comfort of his associates, was anxious to give them recreation whenever possible, and liked nothing better than to amuse and rest himself in their society. Richardson asked a great deal of his assistants from day to day, but they never seemed to think that he asked too much or that they could too eagerly respond to his call. When important work was behind-hand no amount of labor daunted them. When he was on his mettle the office rose to the same pitch of intensity, and when he was rejoicing in some recent triumph his mood was reflected in every face about him. Even those elder pupils who had left him to start upon independent careers did not feel that the connection had really been severed. His office still seemed their professional home and his triumphs their successes, and they were still ready to help him in any emergency.

It is not unimportant to note that courtesy was one of Richardson's weapons of conquest with his subordinates as well as with his friends. Impetuous and imperative though he was at times, he was not imperious to the point of forgetting that his pupils were gentlemen, and did not fail to respect their dignity in his manner of address. When criticising their work he fell into no moods of impatient fault-finding. I have heard more than one man speak of the wonderful patience of this naturally hasty spirit when some one's work had " gone wrong," when some long-considered problem " would not come," when days and weeks had been spent over results which were good for little save to show what must not be done. Instead of saying bluntly that it must not be done he would say, " Let us look into the thing and see what is the matter," and follow up the words with patient criticisms, explanations, hints, and theorizings, so expressed as neither to wound the hearer's feelings nor to damp his courage. An hour's conversation of this sort would leave a beginner inspirited, eager to throw the old work aside and commence again, conscious less of the fact that he had failed than of the fact that now he was going to succeed. Not one or two but many trials were granted him until at last he did succeed; and through them all Richardson's policy would be the same — a policy of confidence, encouragement, and inspiration.

Of course he tried to instill as the basis of every effort a feeling for the primary importance of the problem proposed. Its special intrinsic claims were to be the first things considered, and the precedents of ancient art were to be consulted only for the help they might give towards the free, full, and exact expression of

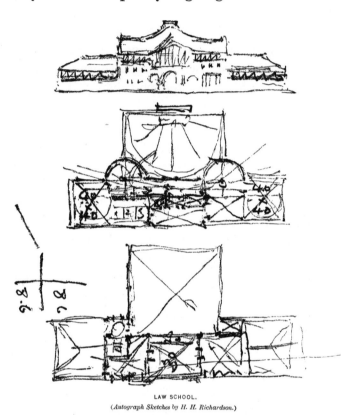

LAW SCHOOL.
(Autograph Sketches by H. H. Richardson.)

these claims. He also insistently recommended his own practice of working even when not actually at work. The habit he had acquired in Paris of first designing in his head and then testing and elaborating upon paper he thought indispensable to an architect. The fact that it saved time was its smallest recommendation. Its greatest was that it fostered a sense of the relative value of chief and minor things; — for a man who begins his design in his head must begin by finding a conception and by arranging principal features; even if he should try he could hardly begin with details.[1]

But the peculiar character of Richardson's teaching is best understood when we learn how near to the bottom of a problem the student was told to begin and how independently he was allowed to attempt its development. The basic conception was always Richardson's own, but the simplest, rudest penciled memoranda conveyed it to his executive. A little rough sketch half the size of his palm (those reproduced in this chapter are characteristic examples) was given to the pupil even though he might be one who had just entered the office. "Do what you can with it," Richardson would say, adding, of course, some general counsels and directions; "Do what you can with it and then we shall see." Then he would not stand at the pupil's elbow to direct his pencil, and would not speedily correct or criticise him, but would wait until he seemed pretty

[1] "I believe," writes a former pupil of Richardson's, "that it was Monsieur André who used sometimes to make his students study a problem without pencil or paper, then get up and describe verbally to him their solutions, and then go to the blackboard and draw out what they had described. If their solutions were not feasible or were not good, the fact became quickly apparent. They began, of course, with simple problems, advancing gradually to the most complicated. This habit, thus early acquired, Mr. Richardson considered of the greatest assistance and value. He has often told me that he did the greater part of his work while driving, or on the cars, or, perhaps, in bed. Sometimes when I have been driving with him he would turn to me and talk of some problem he had in hand just as if he saw it drawn out before him, and discuss various possible solutions of a particular point in the design. He used often to urge upon his pupils the necessity for cultivating the same habit."

well started on the road to success, or found himself in a tight place out of which only the master could help him. Even in the latter case he might get little that was definite from the master except in the way of negative criticism. If a scheme was palpably mistaken he was told to try for another. If a feature evidently would not do Richardson did not exactly prescribe the one which would do. He explained why this one would not, and expected the pupil to put his negative counsel into positive shape. And if he wished to direct him for assistance to historical examples, he did not say " Study this building " or " Adapt that motive," but " In this book or that portfolio you may find something to help you," or, more often, " You had better spend an hour with the photographs." And all this was done with a care and persistence yet a never-flagging fire which drove home the lesson that no time was too much, no pains were too great, to bestow upon the task, and that no task was too difficult to be mastered if due pains and time were given.

Such a method of guidance must often have seemed slow if superficially judged — if judged by its immediate results with regard to the progress of the design which chanced to be in hand. But we know how remarkable was its success in almost every instance, and we can understand how great was its ultimate profit to both master and pupil, — if the pupil had industry, talent, and receptive insight. Richardson did not waste his teaching upon incompetence. Many men benefited by it, but they were all men in whom from the first he had recognized the right sort of ability. If he had not recognized this, or if a novice had failed to win his personal as well as professional interest, a long term might have been spent to little purpose in his office. But pupils whom he liked and in whose talent he believed learned of him as they could have learned of no one else. They learned something very different from the mere power to repeat in careful drawings the careless but comprehensive drawings of another, or to understand definite detailed instructions and reproduce them upon paper. They learned to think for themselves, to design for themselves, to decorate for themselves ; they learned to begin at the beginning and study a thing to the end ; they learned to make a building and not merely to make a drawing. They gained a great share of such experience as our architects most often do not gain until they start independently in their profession ; and they gained it all the better, all the more quickly, by working under supervision. They were not forced to struggle with the vague aims and crude ideals of inexperience, or to criticise their results by its feeble light. The settled aims and the lofty ideals of a great and practiced master were their goal, and though they were often left to discover for themselves a way to reach it, his illuminating criticisms and pregnant hints helped without cramping their efforts.

Nor was Richardson's teaching suspended when he left the draughting-table. He was careful to give his men all the chances he could to increase their general knowledge and develop their taste, and he never talked more or better than when he was among them. The Monday-night dinners which in his later years he organized to bring his actual and his former pupils around him were but the most conspicuous features in an intercourse few moments of which were sterile. His conversation never wandered long from the things he had most at heart, and though it was never didactic it was always doctrinal.   Whether he talked of some special piece of work just then under way, of some still nebulous future scheme, of his own early struggles, of foreign sights, of home necessities, or of the artist's life and tasks in general, he showed the same serious, noble breadth of view, the same enthusiastic, eager, yet reverent spirit.   No man was less of a pedant, and he enjoyed a joke like the youngest; but a jest about art or a light word spoken of the artist's duties hurt him as a joke about religion hurts a devotee.   To Richardson's mind the most important lesson to be taught his pupils was respect for their art and for themselves as its exponents, and the pupil would have been dull indeed who did not learn this at least in the Brookline home.

It seems almost paradoxical that a master could stand so aloof from the task in hand and yet control it so entirely — that pupils could be left so much to themselves and yet do work which was so essentially, thoroughly, individually their master's.   Its aspect is enough to prove that Richardson's work was all his own, in feature and detail no less than in primary conception.   His executives knew it to be so — knew it well at the moment and still better when they came to try to do their own work.   Yet even they could hardly understand and cannot at all explain how it passed from his mind into their minds and hands — by just what process of gradual, imperceptible inoculation.   His fluent, incisive, eager speech, filled with picturesque epithets and piquant illustrations and often tinged with the poetry which is latent in a true artist of any kind, dealt little with particulars, much with generalities, yet in such a way that a sympathetic listener could detect the bearing which these generalities were meant to have upon the particulars before him.   Not many things which the master said could be utilized as precise directions, but everything was rich with meaning from which concrete aid could be extracted.   Even when his hints were vaguest they were vital; even when his suggestions were slightest they were fertile.   Without prescribing a form or dictating a feature he could so talk of the general effect that he wanted to produce, of the bearing of forms and features upon each other, and of the special accent which each should bring into the scheme, that the student would feel in some inexplicable way an exacter meaning than was expressed, and in giving it shape would know that while he seemed to be inventing he was merely translating. Most architects, we are aware, either design a building themselves or hand it over to a subordinate and leave him to deal with it pretty much as he thinks fit; we often see the fact all too clearly expressed in the various structures credited to a single office.   Except in his very early years Richardson never, in the literal sense, designed a building himself.   Yet each building that bears his name was from end to end really his creation.   He developed the individual powers of his pupils, yet moulded them for the time at least into a visible likeness with himself; and he impressed upon them for all time his broad beliefs with regard to the essential virtues which a work of architecture should possess.

Such methods of vicarious yet personal creation and of vague yet pregnant and, in the end, very definite instruction cannot be explained in words.   They were not so much methods of teaching in the usual sense of the term as of inspiration and, so to say, magnetic transmission, and as such are beyond the power of logical thought to analyze or of language fully to record. Their potency and something of their manner of action were recognized, as has been said, for what they were by those who worked in Richardson's office, and could easily be guessed by all others who had come within the influence of his magnetic mind and voice. But some men, doubtless, will find it hard to believe in them, and very few artists can hope to imitate them. Nevertheless, alien though they seem to the mental attitude and the professional customs of our time, there have been times when they must often have been exerted and must have seemed entirely natural. Whenever art has been at its greatest we may divine great artists influencing others in Richardson's way and expressing their own ideas through other hands. To-day each painter, for example, works by and for himself. A picture of Corot's means a picture which no hand but Corot's has touched. A pupil of Meissonier's means a pupil to whom Meissonier is teaching the manipulation of his tools. The followers of Fortuny are a number of independent workers who have seized upon some of his novel ideas or expedients and are trying, each in his own way, to work them out on individual lines. The Impressionist school is a group of artists differing radically among themselves in conception and manner, and merely united in name by certain broad articles of faith — by their approval or disapproval of certain schemes of pictorial interpretation. But if we think of what is meant by a painting of Rubens, by the school of Lionardo, by Perugino's pupils, how great is the contrast! Here we divine methods which may be placed in partial parallel at least with that process of intellectual and emotional influence, of direct inspiration and indirect control, of deputed effort yet personal production, which went on beneath Richardson's roof. It must be confessed, however, that the riddle of how it went on is not thereby clearly read for us.

CHAPTER XX.

INFLUENCE UPON PROFESSION AND PUBLIC.

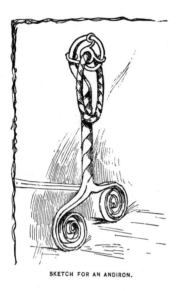

SKETCH FOR AN ANDIRON.

RICHARDSON'S influence upon the members of his profession extended far beyond the walls of his own office, and was both stimulating and ennobling. His success showed that good work might win wide popular appreciation, but that a class of work which had once seemed good enough would not seem so in the future; and the manner in which he had achieved success impressed the lesson that art is a serious matter and should be approached in a serious spirit. Upon the public, too, he exerted a very strong personal influence through contact with clients, friends, and even casual acquaintances. That self-assertion which to some eyes was a fault in his character seems in this connection his greatest merit. Nothing was more to be desired when he began his work than that American architects should have a better chance to show of what they were capable. No champion was more needed than one who should assert their right to do their own work in their own way — should proclaim and prove the fact that an artist knows more about art than the persons who employ him. Richardson's strength of will, directness of aim, genial manner, and beguiling tongue persuaded his clients to give him open opportunities and vigorous backing, to suppress their own crude ideas and wishes, and often to employ him on tasks of a sort for which an artist's help had seldom in the past been thought essential. The result has given us not only his own work but a better chance than we ever had before to get good work from others. In fighting his own battles he fought his comrades' battles, in widening his own path he smoothed and widened theirs, and in guiding and enlightening his clients he leavened the spirit of the whole American public. The unique position which he gained for himself has visibly raised the standing of the architectural profession throughout the whole country. There can be no American city into which some echo of Richardson's

SKETCH FOR AN ANDIRON.

name and fame has not penetrated; and wherever they are even vaguely known the standing and the chances of his humblest brother-artist are thereby improved.

No degree of personal force and charm, however, could by itself have been so

SKETCH FOR AN ANDIRON.

powerful. The influence of Richardson's works upon the general public potently assisted the influence of his words. He was not the first American architect to build good and beautiful structures. But he was the first to build them in a way to attract the eye of every passer, and to win always respectful thought and almost always genuine, hearty admiration. Of all the services Richardson rendered us this is the most important. Of all his legacies the most valuable we possess is a new-born interest in the art of architecture, a growing belief that it may give us true pleasure and that we should therefore try to understand and foster it. The man was made for the place and hour. In other lands those who are capable of learning the value of art are taught by the precepts of long tradition and by the sight of ancient master-pieces. When Richardson began his work our love for art was growing strong but was still crude and ignorant. It was as vague in theory as in practice, and it was not half sure enough of its own value as a factor in national life. An influence like his was what we needed most — an influence which should give both an added impulse to our desires and an increased knowledge of how they might be gratified. Richardson himself knew this and rated his exceptional opportunity at its full worth. Not even his personal fame, dear though it was to him, so touched his imagination and fired his will as the consciousness that this fame was ennobling the attitude of the whole profession towards its work and of the whole public towards the profession.

The impress which Richardson thus made upon his generation has not been beneficial to architecture alone. He knew that architecture as the mother and centre of all other arts and handicrafts should encourage them all for her own sake no less than for theirs. He was among the first American architects to preach and practice the fundamental precept that when walls and roof are standing a building is not finished, but still needs that its builder should concern himself with every detail of its decoration, perfecting it himself or calling upon other artists to perfect it in a way har-

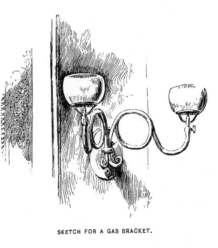

SKETCH FOR A GAS BRACKET.

monious with his own results. No feature was too small, no object too simple to engage his thought. American glass-stainers and decorative painters, architectural carvers in stone and wood, workers in iron and brass, cabinet-makers, carpenters, masons, potters — all to-day do work of a quality for which the last generation might have asked in vain. Those whom Richardson employed profited both intel-

CHAIR IN LIBRARY, MALDEN.

lectually and technically by the nature of the tasks he required and by the wise severity with which he criticised their performance. This was especially the case, of course, with those upon whom he most depended — his carvers and his masons; but a man could not even dig. for Richardson without learning that there was a right way and a wrong way to dig.

Yet though he demanded much of the artisan, and firmly believed that he should be developed into something better than the name had implied in recent years, he was always eager to exchange his help for that of the higher artist. And when an artist's help had been secured, his policy of strict dictation gave place to one of brotherly coöperation. What he wanted was the best work other artists could supply for his particular purpose; and though he insisted that that purpose should be borne in mind, he remembered that what was true of himself was true of others: " No man can do good work who is perpetually cramped and thwarted." From the beginning to the end of his life he was always trying to bring the best sculptors, the best landscape-gardeners, and the best painters of the country into his undertakings; and one of the chief facts which make Trinity Church a mile-stone to mark our progress in art is the fact that it was the first American church the interior decoration of which was intrusted as a whole to a painter of ability.

Neither Richardson's own success nor his public usefulness could have been half so great but for his hearty optimism, synonym as it was for a thorough sympathy with his time and his surroundings. He was successful and influential because his nature was so intensely modern, so thoroughly American. His long familiarity with the triumphs of ancient art had simply inspired the belief that what had been done once could be done again and perhaps improved upon. And his long residence abroad had shown him that opportunities are both freest and richest here, and that latent talent, if not perfected skill, is at least as great. To his mind it argued dullness of vision or weakness of will when an American architect wished he had been born in some other time or land.

There was little in surrounding circumstances or in the cast of Richardson's mind to lead him to talk of the conditions of artistic life in earlier ages. But he often discussed its present conditions in Europe, and always with expressions of thankfulness that his own lines had not been cast there. The priceless teaching of ancient monuments, he thought, could be absorbed by an American, while their distance from his actual place of labor gave him that greatest of all advantages — a free field, an open opportunity. What an architect can do in Europe is largely controlled by the neighborhood of historic works and by the traditions, faiths, and prejudices which antiquarian study has developed. What he can do in America depends only upon himself and upon the sympathy he can awaken in minds which if ignorant are unprejudiced, if untrained are intelligent, if unconscious of their wants are quick to recognize the value of anything which really appeals to them as a combination of good sense and beauty. In Europe a much more intelligent effort is made to secure the best architectural service than has been made in America. But when it is secured it is cramped in ways of which we know nothing — in France by the rule of certain official styles and formulas; in England by the sway of changing fashions, each as insistent for the time as quickly abandoned, and often by the personal ideas of men high in political place; and everywhere by that archæological spirit which demands first of all not that a building shall be sensible and beautiful but that it shall be scholarly, not that it shall represent an artist's own thought but that it shall show his acquaintance with the thought of some forerunner. The greatest difficulty with which our architects have had to contend is public indifference, the greatest with which foreign architects have to contend is public interference, and it is not difficult to see why Richardson thought the former much the smaller hindrance of the two. It seemed to him the one which personal force might more easily overcome in the end and meanwhile might more easily ignore.[1]

His last visit to Paris confirmed this attitude of mind. When he met the friends of his student days he found some of them at the very head of their profession — highly and securely placed, full of work, and rich in honor. But far from envying their position, he regretted that men of such ability should not have the same opportunities that were open to him. He deplored the fact that no one of them was able really to be himself — to discover what he would like best to do in art and then to do it. And when he came home it was with a renewed sense of intense delight in the freedom of his own path, the singleness of his dependence upon a public with fresh eyes and spontaneous instincts.

SKETCH FOR CHAIR IN CAPITOL, ALBANY.

Such feelings may not be shared by men of a different temperament from Richardson's — there is a degree of safety in tradition and prescription which strongly attracts all but the sturdiest spirits. But they were feelings which played a controlling part in his wonderful career. It is not talents or opportunities, he always maintained, which lack in the America of to-day, but merely the will to make good use of them, merely a truer recognition of what art really means and of

---

[1] The history of the Albany Capitol offers, indeed, an instance of public interference with architects' work. But professional voices then incited legislative action, and the case was in every way so exceptional that it does not affect the general contrast between American and European conditions.

what the artist's needs and obligations really are. It was the perception of the fact that these qualities are rapidly developing which made his confidence in the future of American art so great; and it was this confidence, this ever-forward, hopeful gaze, which made him so bold in doing his work and caused him to pursue with pupils, artists, and public alike, that policy of trust, encouragement, and inspiration which has borne such valuable fruit. His creed was the poet's : —

"I know that the past was great and the future will be great,

And that where I am or you are this present day there is the centre of all days, all races,
And there is the meaning to us of all that has ever come of races and days or ever shall come."

Its value as a creed for the American artist may best be judged by its results in Richardson's buildings and in their influence upon the people.

It is difficult to explain why Richardson's work appealed so immediately and so strongly to the public. But the question is of such importance that his biographer cannot escape from the attempt to give at least a partial explanation.

The mere originality of any of his buildings can have had little to do with the matter. Originality of one sort or another has so long been the rule in American architecture that the most striking novelty, if it is nothing more, can hardly excite even a passing curiosity. The solid popular success of Richardson's work — great at once and growing greater year by year — has certainly been due in large degree to those qualities which have already been described as setting it conspicuously apart from modern architectural work in general — to the clearness and vigor of the primary conceptions which it embodies, and to the consistency yet flexibility in matters of treatment which it displays. The strength and clearness of each of Richardson's conceptions attracted the eyes of men whom mere scholarly arrangements of beautiful features or elaborate schemes of decoration left unmoved — putting before them a body which they could not help noticing as a whole and which plainly showed what the aim of the artist had been and what was the nature of his æsthetic ideal. And then his steady yet pliant and sensible adherence to the same ideal in the fulfillment of many different aims impressed its character upon the observer's mind, made him think not of each work by itself but of all together, and thus caused him to realize the difference between an architectural creed and a mere succession of architectural recipes. It was Richardson who first proved to the American public that the speech of a modern architect may be something wholly different from a series of varying quotations or of ever-new inventions — that it may be a consistent yet plastic language, one which inspires the artist yet is ductile in his hands, one which borrows its terms from ancient tongues yet has a thoroughly modern accent and can express a fresh and powerful individuality. It was Richardson who first proved this, and it is not strange, therefore, that he should first have excited a genuine interest in the art he practiced.

A part of the popularity of his works may in this way be explained. But only a part — interest is not necessarily admiration, and they have excited an admiration which seems doubly strong in contrast with the cool indifference that had greeted the best works of his forerunners. This fact is best accounted for, perhaps, by regarding him as the unconscious exponent of an unconscious, latent, yet distinctly marked national taste in architecture. An artist so strong as he would in any case have impressed his generation deeply; but to have made the extraordinary mark he did seems to imply a peculiar concord in feeling between himself and his public.

Upon the question whether this concord was a fact turns the interesting question whether Richardson will be recognized by later generations as the founder and inspirer of a national architectural development. It does not involve the future of his fame as a great artist, or the vitality of his fostering influence upon our love for art in general and our understanding of architectural excellence. These in any case are well assured. And so, we cannot doubt, is the permanence in certain respects of his influence upon the actual character of American architecture. If the collective work of the American architects of to-day is compared with that of fifteen or twenty years ago, the effect of Richardson's example clearly appears; — it would be hard to overstate the degree to which he should receive credit for the growth of this work in vigor, breadth, and simplicity, in coherence and clearness of expression. As far as such qualities as these are concerned his influence must endure. But they are not the only ones in which, at the moment, it is conspicuously embodied. His special schemes and features and types of decoration — his actual creed and style — have found so many adherents that they are fast setting a distinct impress upon the aspect of our towns. We have had many architectural fashions in America but nothing to compare with the vogue of that neo-Romanesque work which often seems to reproduce the true spirit of Richardson's art if at other times it seems merely to imitate or caricature it. And it is the permanence, the spread, the vital development, the eventual triumph in quality and in quantity of this special form of art which are involved in the question whether, in using it, Richardson merely expressed his personal taste or unconsciously expressed the taste of the American people too.

It is not important that we should discuss this question in advance, but it is imperative that we should recognize its exact form and bearing. It cannot be too often repeated that if the renewed Romanesque art which Richardson gave us does in truth continue to grow and flourish, it will not be because he taught us to like it but because when he produced it we liked it by native instinct. This cannot be too often repeated, especially by the young architect for his own guidance. If he clearly understands it he will know that, however great his admiration for Richardson's success, the main thing he has to do is to seek within himself the direction which his own work should take. From the beginning to the end of his career Richardson frankly and emphatically expressed himself, and thus he did the very best that it was possible to do for the great talent which had been given him. It remains for the future to prove whether in expressing himself he really voiced a broad national instinct and thus was fortunate enough to do the best that could possibly be achieved for the art of his country. But no man can help this art or can assist Richardson's influence upon it by trying to work in Richardson's manner unless he feels as clearly as Richardson felt that it is the best manner.

To say this — to say that we should not blindly accept even Richardson as a guide in finding out the things which suit us best in art — is not to impugn his talent or his force. It needed immense talent and force to do what many cannot help believing that he did — clearly to reveal the fact that we had innate artistic tastes. To do more than this — to create tastes — is not within the compass of human power. A man may teach art in one way — by demonstrating its broad principles and by exciting a spirit which shall intelligently appreciate good results of every kind; and in this way Richardson was a very great teacher. But no man ever taught an art, in the sense of prescribing a special manner of practice, except to a people for whom he was the sympathetic spokesman. In fact, the highest praise we can give to an artist is to say that he was his public's spokesman. All narrowly individual merits pale before the great merit of being the one who says first what his fellow-countrymen are eager to hear and thus opens other mouths to give full expression to a national instinct. Not to be isolated but to be representative is to be a true leader, a true creator in art.

Richardson's right to this high title cannot now be decided. But the spirit in which he labored and the work which he produced have already done so much for us, and in the coming years will assuredly do so much more, that we may call him with confidence not only the greatest American artist but the greatest benefactor of American art who has yet been born.

APPENDIX.

———

I.

LIST OF HENRY HOBSON RICHARDSON'S WORKS.

THIS list has been carefully compiled from Richardson's office books, and is believed to be complete. The annexed dates show when the respective commissions were received. In the second division of the list the stars mark the buildings which were independently designed by Mr. Gambrill, all the others having been practically Richardson's own work. In the third division the stars show what buildings were left unfinished at Richardson's death and bequeathed for completion to his successors, Messrs. Shepley, Rutan, and Coolidge.

WORKS BY H. H. RICHARDSON, 111 BROADWAY, NEW YORK.

Church of the Unity, Springfield, Mass.	November, 1866.
Western (now Boston & Albany) R. R. Offices, Springfield, Mass.	1867.
Grace Church, West Medford, Mass.	1867.

WORKS BY GAMBRILL & RICHARDSON, 6 HANOVER STREET AND 57 BROADWAY, NEW YORK.

House for B. W. Crowninshield, Esq., Boston, Mass.	April, 1868.
North Congregational Church, Springfield, Mass.	May, 1868.
House for Wm. Dorsheimer, Esq., Buffalo, N. Y.	October, 1868.
*House for Edward Stimpson, Esq., Dedham, Mass.	October, 1868.
Agawam National Bank, Springfield, Mass.	April, 1869.
*House for Jonathan Sturges, Esq., New York, N. Y.	August, 1869.
High School, Worcester, Mass.	November, 1869.
Exhibition Building, Cordova, Argentine Rep.	February, 1870.
Hotel Brunswick (Alteration), New York, N. Y.	March, 1870.
Brattle Square Church, Boston, Mass.	July, 1870.
State Asylum for the Insane, Buffalo, N. Y.	March, 1871.
Hampden County Court-house, Springfield, Mass.	July, 1871.
Phœnix Insurance Co.'s Building, Hartford, Conn.	March, 1872.
House for F. W. Andrews, Esq., Newport, R. I.	July, 1872.
Trinity Church, Boston, Mass.	July, 1872.
American Merchants' Union Express Co.'s Building, Chicago, Ill.	September, 1872.
House for Benjamin F. Bowles, Esq., Springfield, Mass.	May, 1873.
*House for Dr. J. H. Tinkham, U. S. N., Owego, N. Y.	February, 1874.
House for Wm. Watts Sherman, Esq., Newport, R. I.	September, 1874.
Cheney Building, Hartford, Conn.	September, 1875.
State Capitol, Albany, N. Y.	February, 1876.
Winn Memorial Public Library, Woburn, Mass.	March, 1877.
Ames Memorial Public Library, North Easton, Mass.	September, 1877.

WORKS BY H. H. RICHARDSON, BROOKLINE, MASS.

Sever Hall, Harvard University, Cambridge, Mass.	October, 1878.
Ames Memorial Town Hall, North Easton, Mass.	February, 1879.
Rectory for Trinity Church, Boston, Mass.	April, 1879.

Ames Monument, Sherman, Wyoming Territory . . . . November, 1879.
Gate Lodge for F. L. Ames, Esq., North Easton, Mass. . . . . March, 1880.
Bridge for Department of Public Parks, Boston, Mass. . . . . April, 1880.
Crane Memorial Public Library, Quincy, Mass. . . . . May, 1880.
House for Dr. John Bryant, Cohasset, Mass. . . . . September, 1880.
City Hall, Albany, N. Y. . . . . November, 1880.
Station for Boston & Albany R. R. Co., Auburndale, Mass. . . . . February, 1881.
Austin Hall (Law School), Harvard University, Cambridge, Mass. . . . . . February, 1881.
House for F. L. Higginson, Esq., Boston, Mass. . . . . February, 1881.
House for N. L. Anderson, Esq., Washington, D. C. . . . . May, 1881.
Station for Boston & Albany R. R. Co., Palmer, Mass. . . . . August, 1881.
Pruyn Monument, Rural Cemetery, Albany, N. Y. . . . . October, 1881.
House for Rev. Percy Browne, Marion, Mass. . . . . October, 1881.
Station for Old Colony R. R. Co., North Easton, Mass. . . . . November, 1881.
Dairy Building for Boston & Albany R. R. Co., Boston, Mass. . . . . . . November, 1881.
House for Grange Sard, Jr., Esq., Albany, N. Y. . . . . January, 1882.
Wholesale Store for F. L. Ames, Esq., Kingston and Bedford Streets, Boston, Mass. March, 1882.
Store for F. L. Ames, Esq., Washington Street, Boston, Mass. . . . . . . April, 1882.
House for Mrs. M. F. Stoughton, Cambridge, Mass. . . . . June, 1882.
House for Dr. Walter Channing, Brookline, Mass. . . . . February, 1883.
Billings Library for University of Vermont, Burlington, Vt. . . . . April, 1883.
Station for Boston & Albany R. R. Co., Chestnut Hill, Mass. . . . . . . April, 1883.
Emmanuel Church, Allegheny City, Pa. . . . . August, 1883.
Converse Memorial Public Library, Malden, Mass. . . . . August, 1883.
Station for Boston & Albany R. R. Co., South Framingham, Mass. . . . . . October, 1883.
Station for Connecticut River R. R. Co., Holyoke, Mass. . . . . November, 1883.
*House for Robert Treat Paine, Esq., Waltham, Mass. . . . . January, 1884.
House for John Hay, Esq., Washington, D. C. . . . . January, 1884.
House for Henry Adams, Esq., Washington, D. C. . . . . January, 1884.
*Allegheny County Buildings, Court-house and Jail, Pittsburgh, Pa. . . . . . February, 1884.
Cottage for F. L. Ames, Esq., North Easton, Mass. . . . . March, 1884.
Station for Boston & Albany R. R. Co., Brighton, Mass. . . . . July, 1884.
Baptist Church, Newton, Mass. . . . . October, 1884.
*Station for Boston & Albany R. R. Co., Waban, Mass. . . . . October, 1884.
*Station for Boston & Albany R. R. Co., Woodland, Mass. . . . . October, 1884.
*Station for Boston & Albany R. R. Co., Eliot, Mass. . . . . October, 1884.
House for Prof. E. W. Gurney, Beverly Farms, Mass. . . . . December, 1884.
*House for B. H. Warder, Esq., Washington, D. C. . . . . March, 1885.
Drinking Fountain (for J. J. Bagley Estate), Detroit, Mich. . . . . April, 1888.
*Wholesale Store for Marshall Field, Esq., Chicago, Ill. . . . . April, 1885.
*House for J. J. Glessner, Esq., Chicago, Ill. . . . . May, 1885.
*House for Franklin MacVeagh, Esq., Chicago, Ill. . . . . July, 1885.
Station for Boston & Albany R. R. Co., Wellesley Hills, Mass. . . . . . . July, 1885.
*Chamber of Commerce, Cincinnati, Ohio . . . . August, 1885.
*Union Passenger Station, New London, Conn. . . . . September, 1885.
*House for J. R. Lionberger, Esq., St. Louis, Mo. . . . . November, 1885.
*Armory Building (for J. J. Bagley Estate), Detroit, Mich. . . . . December, 1885.
*House for Prof. Hubert Herkomer, England . . . . January, 1886.
*Store for F. L. Ames, Esq., Harrison Avenue, Boston, Mass. . . . . January, 1886.
*House for Dr. J. H. Bigelow, Newton, Mass. . . . . January, 1886.
*House for Wm. H. Gratwick, Esq., Buffalo, N. Y. . . . . February, 1886.

II.

METHODS OF INSTRUCTION FOLLOWED AND PROBLEMS GIVEN OUT AT THE ECOLE DES BEAUX ARTS, PARIS.

IN explanation of certain references made by Monsieur Gerhardt and by Richardson in their letters from Paris, it may be said that the methods of instruction at the Ecole des Beaux Arts differ in important ways from those followed in our own art schools. In the Architectural Section, as in all the others, the students attend in common upon lectures delivered in the School by various professors. But their practical work is chiefly carried on in *ateliers* which are connected with the School, but only some of which are contained in its building. Certain artists are commissioned by government to direct such studios; and a candidate for admission to the School must belong to one of them, or, at least, must be presented for his entrance examinations by one of their directors — or *patrons*, as they are called.

The sketches for the problems given out from time to time by the Professor of Architecture are made in the *salle de concours* (competition-room) of the School, but are subsequently studied and elaborated in the various *ateliers ;* and then the designs from all the *ateliers* are shown in general competition in the exhibition-galleries of the School. There is, therefore, a double stimulus to exertion in the double rivalry which is excited. Each student contends fraternally against his fellows in his own *atelier ;* yet each feels a strong desire that if no one of the prizes — which except in a few instances are merely honorary — falls to him, something may yet be won by other members of the *atelier*, and his *patron's* reputation as a teacher profit by the fact. So strong, indeed, is this desire, prompted by a generous *esprit de corps*, that individual ambitions are often forgotten, and a student whose own work is already finished, or who has become discouraged over his prospects of success, or whose admiration for some cleverer or pity for some weaker or some tardier brother prompts him to self-sacrifice, will turn from his proper task and give a helping hand elsewhere. A lively series of letters published in "The American Architect and Building News" in 1880 gives an excellent idea of the strenuous, boisterous, rough-and-tumble yet cheerful and fraternal life in these *ateliers*.

The *Prix de Rome* — the most coveted distinction which any student can gain in any modern academy of art — is a prize given every year to the ablest student in each of the sections of the School. It entitles him to four years' free residence at the French Academy of Arts in Rome — the historic Villa Medici — with expenses paid thither and back, and with a stipend which enables him to travel widely during his term. The only obligation is that certain specified pieces of work must be sent to Paris at certain specified intervals of time and must remain the property of the government. Moreover, a winner of the *Prix de Rome*, when his term is over, is given immediate employment under government and, of course, is exceptionally well launched in life by the mere fact of having attained the academic distinction. The competitions for this prize are specially conducted, are very severe, and are open to French citizens only. All the other privileges and honors of the School, however, are freely and impartially conferred upon men of every nation.

Several circulars for the ordinary School competitions were found among Richardson's papers, and two of them are here translated in full to give an idea of the kind of work demanded and of the manner in which it is required to be executed. It may be remarked that neither in the more elementary nor in the more advanced competition is any perspective drawing desired.

The first circular reads as follows : —

IMPERIAL SCHOOL OF FINE ARTS. ARCHITECTURAL SECTION. SECOND CLASS.

PROBLEM FOR THE COMPETITION OF JUNE 3, 1863.

The Professor of Theory proposes as the subject of competition : A Casino, over a thermal mineral spring.

This Casino, erected on the promenade of one of our great thermal establishments, is to cover a spring the medicinal qualities of which permit only the drinking of the water.

As the drinkers who will frequent it must find places for recreation and for study, it shall be composed as follows : —

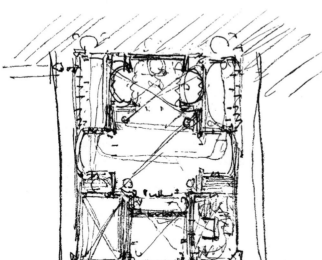

AUTOGRAPH SKETCH BY H. H. RICHARDSON, ON MARGIN OF CIRCULAR RELATING TO CASINO COMPETITION.

Ground-Floor :

A vestibule.

A general assembly-room where will be the fountain, and benches or *exedras* for conversation.

A billiard-room.

One or two staircases.

Covered promenades.

All to be adorned with statues and other works of art.

Second Floor :

A room for retirement and study.

A loggia open towards the promenade.

Terraces ornamented with flowers.

The site occupied by the building shall not exceed thirty meters in greatest dimension.

To be presented as sketches :

General plan of the ground floor ; half plan of second floor ; elevation and section, to the scale of .005 per meter.

As drawings :

The two plans, in entirety, to a scale of one centimeter per meter ; elevation and section to double this scale. The construction to be indicated in the section.

(Signed) Le Sueur.

Paris, *June* 3, 1863.

The second circular is dated two years later, but bears neither heading nor professor's signature. It was evidently given out to a higher class than the other, as the problem it presents is of far greater difficulty.

A PREPARATORY SCHOOL OF MEDICINE, WITH A CLINICAL HOSPITAL ATTACHED, FOR THE CHIEF TOWN OF A DEPARTMENT.

This establishment, destined in part for the teaching of medicine and in part for the treatment of a limited number of patients, shall consist of but a single edifice, yet shall preserve in each of its main divisions — school and hospital — the character appropriate thereto.

The edifice shall be composed of,

On the Ground-Floor :

1st. A rather large vestibule preceding a lecture-room capable of holding two hundred students. The dependencies of this room shall be : An office for the professors ; one or two rooms for anatomical preparations ; a chemical laboratory ; a pharmacy ; a room for the collection of surgical instruments. All these to be more rather than fewer in number.

2d. A small library to serve as a study.

3d. A museum of anatomy.

4th. Janitor's and secretary's rooms.

5th. A ward for twenty male patients suffering from complaints which need surgical attention.

6th. Ditto for male children ditto.

7th. Ditto for female patients ditto.

8th. Ditto for female children ditto.

9th. A very large kitchen with all appurtenances.

10th. Offices for gratuitous consultations.

11th. Several rooms for patients with contagious diseases.

12th. A bath-room.

13th. A reception-room for patients.

14th. A mortuary chamber.

15th. A small chapel.

16th. A janitor's room and an administration-room with living-rooms above.

17th. A large and commodious stairway giving access to the second floor.

The second floor as well as the third shall be devoted to wards for patients, — men, women, and children, — of whom the total number is not to exceed one hundred and sixty for both floors, divided as nearly as possible twenty to a ward, and to accommodations for fifteen Sisters of Charity and as many resident students. The attics to be devoted to servants' quarters.

The building shall have two entirely distinct entrances, — that of the school to face the north and that of the hospital the south. The site, including the gardens, is not to exceed ninety thousand square meters in extent, and shall be contained between two boundary walls, one towards the west, the other towards the east. An isolated site must be reserved for a pavilion for dissecting purposes.

Facade, section, and plan to a scale of .002.

Certain parts of this composition must be monumental without exaggeration. Other parts, on the contrary, must be of great simplicity without coldness. Cheerfulness rather than sombreness of effect is to be aimed at, in order that the patient may not enter with regret.

February, 1865.

III.

EXTRACTS FROM RICHARDSON'S DESCRIPTION OF TRINITY CHURCH.

. . . On testing the ground at the site a compact stratum was found, overlaid by a quantity of alluvium, upon which a mass of gravel, about thirty feet deep, had been filled in. Upon such a foundation was to be built a structure, the main feature of which consisted in a tower weighing nearly nineteen million pounds, and supported on four piers. The first pile was driven April 21, 1873. Every pile was watched, numbered, its place marked on a plan at a large scale, and a record made of the weight of the hammer with which it was driven, the distance that the pile sank at the last three blows, and the height from which the hammer fell. With these indications, a map of the bearing stratum was made, with contour lines, showing the surface of the clay bed. . . .

On the 10th of October, 1873, the contract was made with Messrs. Norcross Brothers, of Worcester, Mass., for the masonry and carpenter-work of the structure; the building-committee, who had a large quantity of stone on the ground brought from the ruins of the Summer Street Church, undertaking to furnish all the foundation stone, except that for the great piers of the tower, which it was necessary to construct of special stones. Under the centre of the church a space ninety feet square had been reserved for the tower foundation, and this had been driven uniformly full of piles, as near together as practicable, over two thousand being contained in the area. This area, while the foundation walls for the other parts of the church were building, was subjected to various processes, in preparation for its future duty.

The piles within these limits were cut off at "grade five," six inches lower than the piles under the other portions of the building, as an excess of precaution against any failure of water for keeping the wood saturated. The ground was then excavated around the heads of the piles to a depth of two feet, and replaced with concrete. The concrete was mixed on the ground, put into barrows, and wheeled on plank-ways laid on the heads of the piles to its destination, and thrown into the excavation. Four successive layers, each six inches thick, were put in, and each was thoroughly compacted with wooden rammers. The upper surface of the concrete was kept one inch below the heads of the piles, on the theory that the piles being the true support of the structure, it was important that every stone should rest firmly upon them, without coming in contact with the concrete, which might some time sink, by the settlement of the gravel filling, and cause dislocation of any masonry which might rest partly upon it and partly on the unyielding piles. The concrete, however, had an important use in preventing the lateral motion of the piles, and to some exent connecting them together.

Before the close of this season, the first course of one of the four pyramids which form the foundation of the tower piers had been laid on the piles, and as an experiment the outside joints were cemented up, and the whole was then grouted with cement and sand till the joints and the space between the stone and concrete were flushed full. The pumping, which had been constantly kept up to free the excavation from the water which came in through the gravelly bottom, then ceased, and the water was allowed to enter the cavity, which it soon filled to the depth of about four feet, and the operations on the ground were suspended until the following spring. . . .

On resuming operations in the spring of 1874, it was found that the tide water, coming in through the gravel, had affected the setting of the cement. The concrete was in a favorable condition, but the grouting of the masonry which had been started for the piers was still very soft, although made with a cement which, under ordinary circumstances, sets rapidly. In view of this unexplained difficulty, as well as the need of proceeding rapidly with the piers without being obliged to wait for the setting of any doubtful cement, it was thought best to reduce the matter to certainty by using Portland cement throughout the piers. A variety of English and French Portland cements was tried, but the result seemed equally good with all, some difference in the rapidity of setting being the principal variation. The stones already set were taken up and relaid, and with the substitution of the different cement, treated as before ; the outer joints being packed close, and the inside grouted until completely full.

At first the Portland cement was handled like Rosendale in similar circumstances, the cement being mixed rather dry, and after being put into the joints with trowels, compressed as much as possible with rammers ; but further experience and careful trials showed equally good results by first filling the larger joints with a trowel and the drier mortar, and then mixing some rather rich cement, sufficiently liquid to pour into the smaller joints from a bucket, stirring it well with the thicker portion, until the whole was of a medium consistency and had penetrated into every interstice of the stone-work. Each course was leveled up to a uniform surface with cement, and chips where necessary, before the next course was begun, and the upper bed of the third course from the top, and all the vertical and horizontal joints of the two upper courses were taken out of wind and pointed, so as to form a perfectly close joint.

Toward the close of 1874, the four pyramids of solid granite, each thirty-five feet square at the base and seven feet square at the top, and seventeen feet high, were completed ; the main walls of the church being then well advanced, and the chapel, which had been urged forward with great rapidity, nearly finished. . . .

During the winter, the stone for the remainder of the building was cut, the larger portion of the work being upon the granite for the upper part of the piers which carry the tower. These were blocks of Westerly granite, each five feet by two and one-half, and twenty inches high, with hammered vertical and horizontal joints. These were laid in cement, in pairs, forming a pillar five feet square in section, the joints of alternate courses crossing. For laying these piers and the adjoining walls, as well as the arches between the piers, a massive scaffold was built, standing independently upon the four pyramids of the tower foundation. Four derricks stood upon this structure, and not only the pier stones, weighing two tons each, were easily handled, but the same stage served afterward to carry the centres for the great arches, and the whole superstructure of scaffolding, to the very top of the tower, no outside staging being used. This " great stage," as it was called, remained in place for more than two years.

In the construction of the great arches and for tying the piers at the summit to the walls of the nave and transept iron was used, but sparingly, and as a matter of precaution rather than necessity, the weights and points of application of the adjoining walls having been calculated to furnish sufficient resistânce to the thrust of the arches without the aid of ties. In general, throughout the building, the use of iron was avoided as far as might be, and with the exception of the staircase turret, which is supported by a double set of iron beams over the vestibule below, no masonry in the church is dependent on metal for support. . . .

IV.

EXTRACTS FROM MEMORANDA AND LETTERS RELATING TO THE CATHEDRAL DRAWINGS.

EXTRACTS FROM RICHARDSON'S MEMORANDA SUBMITTED WITH THE DRAWINGS.

. . . ENTERING the church by the western porches, one finds on the left of the ample vestibules the baptistry, a vaulted polygonal apartment somewhat more than eighteen feet in diameter, having the font in the centre. . . . On the right, and corresponding with the baptistry, is a grand staircase leading to the gallery over the western vestibules. Smaller spiral staircases lead to the smaller galleries over the transept entrances, and still smaller ones on the western front lead to the triforium galleries. . . . Besides the great western porches and the transept porches, cloister entrances are provided which give that protection from the weather so necessary in our climate. . . . The vestries for the bishop, the clergy and the choir are placed in chambers whose circular form, subdivided as shown on the plan, makes them especially well adapted to the purpose for which they are designed. These rooms are reached by the ambulatory which runs around the apse and which is divided off by a wrought-iron screen, so as to give a retired communication to the vestries while leaving the arcades perfectly open and thus not interfering with the grandeur of the design. These ambulatories are filled with light from the windows above the roofs of the vestries all around the apse. . . .

It is proposed to build the church of some warm granite with Longmeadow brown sandstone, the roofs of the towers to be of stone, the other roofs of slate. Messrs. Norcross Brothers' estimate includes everything to complete the church as shown in the drawings, with all stained-glass windows, carvings and sculpture, and all furniture shown in drawings. . . .

The bid of Messrs. Norcross Brothers for the temporary cathedral includes the foundations of the vaulted tower weighing twenty thousand tons. These foundations will be nearly one hundred feet square, of the best granite, laid in a bed of concrete. This bid includes also the clerestory walls, which are the highest in the church (except the gable walls), and also the seats and other necessary furniture, and, in short, a temporary church as shown in the plans complete for use in every particular. This temporary church is so arranged that the progress of the work in the rest of the cathedral can proceed without in any way disturbing the services of the church in the temporary structure except for a short interval when the roof will have to be pierced to carry up the piers and walls.

EXTRACTS FROM LETTER TO THE BISHOP OF THE DIOCESE OF ALBANY, MARCH 30, 1883.

In the interior [of the completed structure] (as shown in the section) the arches of the triforium are open with a passage between them and the wall, and in the clerestory is a similar passage, so that the clerestory windows are seen through these open arches. . . .

The main walls of the church which measure six feet thick on plan are, for the sake of economy, to be built hollow. They have to be made as thick as six feet on account of the passages above. These walls would be built eighteen inches thick outside, eighteen inches thick inside, with a hollow space of three feet in the middle, the two walls being securely tied together at proper intervals. The walls of my design (both the clerestory and the aisle walls), if measured, will be found not very high, nor are the western towers of great height, but kept within bounds in order to give greater value and interest to the main feature of the composition, the great, many-sided central tower crowning and dominating the whole mass.

With regard to the temporary structure, I would add that it is proposed to carry out the central portion of the completed plan as the temporary church, carrying up the piers as far as to the top of their capitals, and surrounding the whole by a temporary thin brick wall which could be easily taken down when the great church outside of it is completed.

The bid for the temporary structure includes, as was said, the massive foundations of the great tower and of the highest walls of the church. My experience with the uncertain soil of Albany, which has been somewhat extensive, has led me to see the necessity of treating these foundations with the greatest care. For this reason the greater part of the one hundred and fifty thousand dollars allotted for the temporary building would have to be in any case put below ground. And I have taken great care to reduce the height of my walls, both of nave and chancel, to a minimum size consistent with largeness of effect. I beg that you and the chapter will give particular consideration to the estimates; for however much I should like to make you a more attractive offer, I feel that the bid for the temporary structure is as low as it could be consistent with thorough workmanship.

If the interior of the cathedral is made of brick with a cement surface, only the piers, arches, vaulting-ribs, and mouldings being of stone, the whole building can be completed within one million dollars. This would give a great opportunity for a magnificent treatment of the interior in color — a treatment at least as noble as could be made in stone, and one which is especially adapted to our climate, which, with its long winter of five months, seems to call for warm and cheerful interiors glowing with color. Nor can anything be more imposing and solemn, more truly religious in sentiment, than a great church-interior appropriately decorated in color, as is well known to any one familiar with the church of St. Mark at Venice; and indeed such a treatment is supported by the precedent of many of the noblest church-interiors of Europe. A color treatment on a cement surface has also this advantage; that, while the interior can be agreeably and cheaply finished at once, it gives opportunity for adding from time to time to the decorations as funds are given for the purpose, and thus the interior grows in richness and beauty, solemnity and significance.

As, however, in the conditions no sum is mentioned as the limit of cost of the completed design, I most respectfully claim that the architect should be chosen solely with reference to the merits of his design as fulfilling in the best way the conditions propounded. If the chapter then desire to limit the cost of the completed design, the chosen architect can so modify his design as to meet this new condition, or submit, if necessary, a new design whose cost shall be within the sum they decide upon.

In conclusion I should like to say a word with regard to the effects I have aimed at in my design. In the first place I have tried to avoid making my cathedral merely an enlarged parish church. And I have striven to give the church that dignity and strength, that calmness and repose which should be the attributes of a great cathedral. These qualities, it seemed to me, could only be obtained by the most carefully studied proportion of parts and masses, by the greatest simplicity of form and treatment, — for grandeur is always characterized by simplicity, — and by unity of design, to obtain which I have used one consistent treatment around the whole structure, interior and exterior, carrying some strong features around the whole building, tying it together, as it were, with great bands, while not neglecting to give to the different parts of the cathedral that distinctive treatment which they seemed to demand.

EXTRACTS FROM LETTER OF THE BISHOP OF THE DIOCESE OF ALBANY TO RICHARDSON, MAY 6, 1883.

. . . Apart from all other considerations, the great expense of the completed building and the unsatisfactoriness of the temporary structure made the acceptance of the plans impossible.

Even the suggestion of an interior finishing in plaster and colors (to which I could never consent) would have left too great an expense. What I wanted to say to you . . . was to thank you for your interest in the matter, to assure you that your enthusiasm has inspired us with a new feeling of interest and admiration for you and your work, and to add that while I consider the plans which we have accepted better suited to the cathedral worship of the Episcopal Church and more adapted to our needs in Albany, I recognize the dignity of your design, with most of whose leading features I am thoroughly in sympathy. I trust the opportunity may offer for its carrying out elsewhere. . . .

V.

H. H. RICHARDSON'S PROFESSIONAL CIRCULAR FOR INTENDING CLIENTS; USED DURING THE LATTER PART OF HIS LIFE.

Dear Sir: The following statement was prepared in reply to the request of a client for an explanation of the basis of my charges, and of the responsibilities which, as an architect, I undertake: —

It has been my practice to charge five per cent. on the cost of the building, with an additional charge, which covers: 1st, the visits of the clerk of the work; 2d, his traveling expenses; 3d, my time lost in traveling; 4th, my traveling expenses.

My habit at one time was to charge for these by items, but I found this was as annoying to my clients as to myself, and I now prefer to charge a fixed commission of eight per cent. for all work costing more than ten thousand dollars, unless the work is so far distant that the extra charge of three per cent. will not cover loss of time and traveling expenses.

When interior work, such as mantels, wainscoting, ceilings, carving on walls, columns, etc., is done separately, the charge is very much higher than five per cent., sometimes as high as fifty per cent. But the charge of eight per cent. covers everything inside and out that is not movable furniture. I undertake, by myself, or my clerk of the works, to see that all the necessary supervision is given to the building. The duration and extent of such supervision will be determined by the nature and character of the work. I do not agree to supervise, for instance, the laying of each brick or the driving of each nail, but I do agree to exercise such supervision as is calculated to, and ordinarily will, secure the furnishing of materials of the kind and quality required by the contract, and the performance of the work in accordance with the plans and specifications, and in a good, workmanlike, and substantial manner.

In so far as concerns the plans and specifications, I guarantee that the building, when erected in accordance therewith, shall be suited to the uses for which it is erected, and that the specification shall embrace all that will be required to completely finish it, unless it shall have been otherwise expressly understood between the owner and myself.

For any errors of construction which appear on my plans, or for any failure to properly supervise the work, whereby the building, when completed, is rendered insecure or unsafe, or the stories or rooms are made inaccessible or incapable of being devoted to the uses for which the plans showed they were intended, I consider myself responsible.

In preparing the architectural design, I agree, after consultation with the owner, to use my best judgment. I cannot, however, guarantee that the building, when completed, shall conform to his ideas of beauty or taste, or indeed to those of any person or school. I can only agree to examine and consider this matter well and carefully, and to recommend nothing which is inconsistent with my own ideas upon these subjects.

Of course, when I follow the owner's positive instructions, I consider myself relieved from all responsibility whatsoever.

Yours very truly,

H. H. RICHARDSON.

INDEX.